MW00889987

Oahu Travel and Adventure Guide

The Ultimate Shortcut to Thrills, Beauty, and Culture, and Authentic Experiences

Ocean Breeze Adventures

Contents

Copyright © 2024 by Ocean Breeze Adventures

All rights reserved.

No portion of this book may be reproduced in any form without written permission from the publisher or author, except as permitted by U.S. copyright law.

This publication is designed to provide accurate and authoritative information in regard to the subject matter covered. It is sold with the understanding that neither the author nor the publisher is engaged in rendering legal, investment, accounting or other professional services. While the publisher and author have used their best efforts in preparing this book, they make no representations or warranties with respect to the accuracy or completeness of the contents of this book and specifically disclaim any implied warranties of merchantability or fitness for a particular purpose. No warranty may be created or extended by sales representatives or written sales materials. The advice and strategies contained herein may not be suitable for your situation. You should consult with a professional when appropriate. Neither the publisher nor the author shall be liable for any loss of profit or any other commercial damages, including but not limited to special, incidental, consequential, personal, or other damages.

Book Cover by NabPerfect

Illustrations by [Illustrator]

1st edition 2024

Oahu Hawai'i

May there always be warmth in your heart, fish in your net, and Aloha in your heart. —Unknown

In the heart of the Pacific Ocean lies a maze of islands adorned with lush landscapes, vibrant cultures, and a spirit that whispers of ancient wisdom. Picture yourself standing on a sun-kissed shore, the rhythmic melody of waves serenading your soul as the salty breeze weaves through your hair. In this moment, you feel a deep connection to the land, a sensation as timeless as the islands themselves.

But amidst the swaying palms and cascading waterfalls lies a tale of resilience, tradition, and the ever-present spirit of Aloha. Welcome to a journey through the enchanting realm of Hawaii, where every sunrise paints a new story and every sunset whispers secrets of the past. Join us as we dive into the depths of this paradise, uncovering its hidden gems, embracing its cultural tapestry, and igniting the flame of Aloha within our hearts. For in this land of warmth, wonder, and eternal Aloha, every moment is a treasure waiting to be discovered.

Here's why you should pack your bags and embark on an unforgettable adventure:

- **Rich culture:** Immerse yourself in the tapestry of Hawaiian culture on Oahu. From the historic landmarks that echo with ancient tales to the hands-on traditional activities that connect you with the island's roots, Oahu is a cultural haven. Don't forget to indulge your taste buds in the unique and diverse food scene that reflects the island's heritage.

- **Lively atmosphere:** Known as "the gathering place," Oahu thrives with energy and life. The island's vibrant environment and diverse population combine to offer a unique tropical vacation experience. Feel the pulse of the island as you explore bustling markets, lively events, and the welcoming spirit of its people.

- **Beautiful beaches:** Oahu's shores are a canvas of breathtaking beauty. Whether you seek the thrill of water activities or dream of unwinding on soft sands, the island's beaches cater to every beachgoer's paradise. Dive into the Pacific, catch a wave, or simply bask in the sun—Oahu's beaches offer a slice of heaven for everyone.

- **Diverse dining:** Prepare your taste buds for a culinary journey. Oahu's dining scene is a melting pot of flavors, blending local ingredients with international influences. From humble food trucks to upscale restaurants, the island caters to all tastes and budgets, ensuring that every meal is a delightful adventure.

- **Interesting landmarks and attractions:** Oahu is a treasure trove of wonders. Explore natural marvels, delve into history at iconic landmarks, and witness the island's charm unfold. Whether hiking to panoramic vistas or discovering the tales behind historical sites, Oahu promises a diverse range of attractions for every kind of explorer.

- **Accessibility and convenience:** As the home of Honolulu, Oahu strikes the perfect balance between city life and natural beauty. With easy accessibility, the island invites you to explore both its bustling urban hubs and serene landscapes, creating a seamless fusion of convenience and adventure.

- **Local experience:** Venture beyond the tourist hotspots to discover the heartbeat of Oahu. Experience the everyday life of the island, immerse yourself in local communities, and explore the less crowded, more authentic corners of Oahu. Live like a local and let the island reveal its hidden gems.

- **Diverse activities:** Oahu is a playground for the adventurous. Hike through lush landscapes, snorkel in crystal-clear waters, ride the waves on renowned surf breaks, and indulge in retail therapy in vibrant shopping districts. Whatever your idea of the perfect vacation, Oahu offers a diverse array of activities to create your dream getaway.

- **Cosmopolitan and charming:** Oahu's cosmopolitan flair is seamlessly woven into its charming towns and natural wonders. Whether strolling through lively urban streets or discovering hidden gems in quaint neighborhoods, the island's blend of sophistication and allure captivates every traveler.

- **Aloha spirit:** More than a greeting, the Aloha spirit is a way of life on Oahu. The warmth and welcoming nature of the island's residents create an atmosphere where visitors feel not just like guests but like family. Let the Aloha spirit embrace you, leaving you with cherished memories that linger long after you've bid farewell to Oahu.

Let's talk about the struggles and roadblocks that might make planning your Oahu adventure feel like navigating through a maze. Because, let's face it, the journey to a dream vacation isn't always smooth sailing. We get it, and we've heard your concerns.

Picture this: you arrive on Oahu, excited to immerse yourself in the local culture, only to find yourself trapped in touristy areas. The frustration is real—that deep-seated yearning for authentic, off-the-beaten-path experiences. You crave more than surface-level encounters; you want to feel the pulse of Oahu, connect with its people, and create memories that go beyond the typical tourist script.

The internet, a vast ocean of information, can quickly turn into a storm of confusion. Planning an itinerary becomes a daunting task as you navigate through countless options. The anxiety creeps in; decision fatigue sets in. How do you ensure your time on Oahu is well-spent when every choice seems equally enticing? It's like standing at a buffet with too many delicious options, and suddenly, the joy of planning morphs into an overwhelming burden.

The conscientious traveler in you raises concerns about your impact on the beautiful destinations you love. The guilt is palpable—every step, every choice, weighs on your mind. Can you truly enjoy your adventure when the environment suffers? The conflict is real, and the desire to explore responsibly tugs at your heartstrings.

Life is fast-paced, and your schedule is packed. Researching and planning a vacation seems like a luxury, one you can't afford. The fear of missing out on hidden gems and unique experiences nags at you. The clock is ticking, and the pressure to make the most of your limited vacation time adds an extra layer of stress.

The fear of missing out is a modern-day traveler's dilemma. What if there's a hidden gem, an extraordinary experience, waiting just around the corner? The anxiety of not making the most of your Oahu adventure looms large, threatening to overshadow the joy of exploration.

Finances are the silent hurdle standing between you and premium experiences. The disappointment is tangible—the feeling of missing out on something extraordinary because the budget doesn't stretch that far. How do you balance your desire for exclusive activities with the constraints of your wallet?

Safety is paramount, especially when venturing into new territories. For solo travelers or those exploring with families, personal safety is a top concern. Anxiety and fear taint the joy of exploration, making one wonder if the destination is actually worth the risk.

You yearn for more than a superficial encounter with Oahu. The lack of a meaningful connection with the destination and its people leaves a void. It's not just about ticking off landmarks; it's about feeling the soul of Oahu, creating a bond that lingers long after you've left.

Understanding and respecting local customs and traditions can be tricky. The discomfort of being unsure and the fear of unintentionally disrespecting the very essence of Oahu—it's a struggle. How do you bridge the gap and navigate a new culture with grace?

Moments slip through your fingers like grains of sand, and capturing the essence of your Oahu adventure becomes a challenge. The frustration of not being able to relive and share those unique moments weighs heavy on your heart.

We get it—the journey to Oahu is not just about the destination; it's about overcoming these hurdles and creating an experience that resonates with you. Let's navigate this together and ensure your Oahu adventure is everything you've dreamt of and more.

Imagine this: You're sitting at your desk, staring at a screen flooded with countless tabs of travel guides and forums, each promising the ultimate Oahu experience.

Your mind races with questions: Where do I begin? How do I ensure an authentic adventure without falling into tourist traps? Will I truly connect with the essence of Oahu amidst the chaos of choices?

That overwhelming feeling, that knot of uncertainty in your stomach, is the catalyst that brought you here. You crave a solution, a guide that understands your struggles and simplifies your journey.

This book is your compass through the maze of options, offering shortcuts to the heart of Oahu. Inside, you'll find curated itineraries that capture the island's essence, insider tips to unlock hidden gems, and practical advice to navigate local customs effortlessly. Say goodbye to decision fatigue and hello to authentic, meaningful experiences that resonate long after your journey ends.

As the authority on Adventuring Oahu, Ocean Breeze Adventures is renowned for our dedication to unlocking the island's enchanting world. With a mission to inspire and guide fellow adventure enthusiasts, we navigate the vibrant land-scapes, hidden gems, and thrilling experiences Oahu offers.

Passionate about Oahu's natural beauty and cultural richness, we believe in cre-ating unforgettable memories while respecting the island's heritage and envi-ronment. Our "Adventuring Oahu" book caters to diverse adventurers, ensuring everyone finds their perfect guide.

Rooted in responsible tourism, we encourage sustainable practices, leaving a positive impact on the island and its people. Join Ocean Breeze Adventures on a journey to unlock Oahu's secrets while fostering a deep appreciation for its treasures.

Adventure awaits—come explore Oahu with us!

Chapter One

Aloha Waikiki

Hawaii is not a state of mind, but a state of grace. —Paul Theroux

I n this chapter, we'll take a look at the essence of Oahu, a captivating canvas where lush landscapes, vibrant cultures, and endless adventures converge. From the towering peaks of Diamond Head to the rhythmic hula by the shores, Oahu beckons you on an extraordinary journey. So, kick off your shoes, feel the warm sand between your toes, and let's set off on a captivating exploration of Oahu, your gateway to unforgettable escapes.

Section 1: Getting Here

Let's start by gathering all the information you need to know to get here.

Choosing Your Arrival Point

Before you begin your Oahu adventure, figuring out your arrival point is definitely the first step. The Daniel K. Inouye International Airport (HNL), fondly known as Honolulu International Airport, is the largest airport in Hawaii and is usually the first option for many (Airport Info, n.d.). It's situated in Honolulu, and it connects Oahu with numerous flights to Asia, North America, and Oceania.

Non-stop departures from HNL cover a wide range of cities, including Sydney, Chicago, Atlanta, Houston, Portland, Oakland, New York, Seoul, Kansai, Manila, and so on (Airport Info, n.d.). Hawaiian Airlines, with a bustling hub at the airport, is the largest airline that's serving HNL.

Whether you are hopping between the islands or coming from a farther destination, layovers and connecting flights at HNL are completely hassle-free. Here are some helpful tips for you:

- Use online tools like AirNav or other search engines for a smoother experience in finding the best connecting flights.

- Always double-check layover times to ensure they strike a balance between your schedule and comfort level.

- HNL boasts plenty of amenities that you can explore during your layover, like lounges, restaurants, and shops.

- There are plenty of information screens and signage spread across airport premises, but you need to be wary of any sudden changes.

Navigating Customs and Immigration

Just like every other country, there are some entry requirements and documentation you need to be aware of before you can enter Hawaii. Here's a brief overview:

- **Visa requirements:** If you are a U.S. citizen traveling to Hawaii, you will not require a visa because Hawaii is included within the United States. However, citizens from other countries will have to apply for a visa, and you can check your visa requirements based on your citizenship through the official U.S. government website.

- **Passport:** US citizens do not need a passport to enter Hawaii, just your Driver's license. Be aware starting May 7, 2025 a _REAL ID_ will be needed. Visitors from outside the US will need a valid passport.

- **Visa Waiver Program (VWP):** Citizens from certain countries are eligible under the VWP whereby they don't need a visa to enter Hawaii. But before boarding their flights, they should apply for authorization through the Electronic System for Travel Authorization, or ESTA.

- **Customs information:** You must gain some knowledge about the customs regulations of the country if you want a smooth entry. Take note of restrictions regarding agricultural products, plants, or foods.

- **Customs Declaration Form:** You will receive a Customs Declaration Form before entering Hawaii that you need to fill out as accurately as you can because you need to provide information on items that you are bringing into the country.

- **Immigration Form:** You may also have to fill out an immigration form. Ensure that you fill it out accurately.

For a smooth customs process, keep these tips in mind:

- Research the rules and regulations of the country, especially regarding any agricultural items or plants that you are bringing.

- Keep all your essential documents, like your passport and vessel registration, handy for inspection.

- Beware of the restricted items in the country, and in case you are carrying them, declare them beforehand.

- If you don't want delays in customs clearance, make sure your invoices are accurate and up-to-date.

- For a smooth customs inspection process, it is necessary to seal your freight properly.

- To steer clear of customs issues, research a bit about the country's shipping laws.

- During the customs inspection, be prepared for the common questions they might ask.

- If this is your first time, it's better you take the help of a shipping company experienced in handling the process for a hassle-free customs clearance.

In order to protect the unique ecosystem of Hawaii, the Hawaii Department of Agriculture (HDOA) has strict rules regarding what items you can carry into the country. The introduction of even one invasive pest or disease can be disastrous. So, make sure you stay updated on what items you can bring in and out of the state.

Information for Canadian Citizens

For Canadian citizens entering the United States, the primary requirement is to provide proof of Canadian citizenship for which you obviously need your passport along with a few other documents (International Travelers, n.d.).

By air: If you are coming to Hawaii by air, you should produce your passport or your NEXUS card throughout the duration of your stay. Temporary passport holders may encounter different entry requirements, and official passport holders should refer to the Official Travel page for potential variations.

By water (cruise): In accordance with the Western Hemisphere Travel Initiative (WHTI), Canadian citizens aged 16 and above must provide one of the following documents for U.S. entry by land or water:

- Passport

- NEXUS card

- Free and Secure Trade (FAST) card

- Enhanced driver's license (EDL) or enhanced identification card (EIC) from a province or territory with an implemented U.S.-approved EDL/EIC program

- Secure Certificate of Indian Status

The chosen WHTI-compliant document must remain valid for the entire U.S. stay. For those aged 15 and under entering the U.S. by land or water, proof of citizenship like a passport, original or copy of a birth certificate, or an original Canadian citizenship card is required. Travelers aged 18 and under, accompanied by a school or organized group under adult supervision, must also present proof of citizenship.

For the use of a Secure Certificate of Indian Status as an entry ID, additional information can be found on the Citizenship and Immigration Services (USCIS) and Indigenous and Northern Affairs Canada websites. Canadian permanent residents of the U.S. must adhere to specific entry requirements, detailed on the CBP website.

Visas: In general, Canadian citizens do not need a visa to enter the U.S. directly from Canada for visits or studies.

Length of stay: Canadian citizens, including "snowbirds" wintering in the U.S., are typically granted a stay of up to six months upon entry. The duration is determined by a Customs and Border Patrol (CBP) officer at the port of entry based on the purpose of travel. If a longer stay is desired, an extension must be applied for with the nearest USCIS office before the initial authorized stay expires.

Dual citizenship: For Canadians with both U.S. and Canadian citizenship, presenting a valid U.S. passport is mandatory for air travel. Although not formally required, carrying both passports can facilitate entry into the U.S. and return to Canada.

Section 2: What to Bring

Here's a breakdown of crucial packing essentials:

Clothing Recommendations Based on Season

Tailor your wardrobe to the season with lightweight and wrinkle-proof fabrics. For the warm summer months (June–October), pack shorts, t-shirts, tank tops, and a sarong for versatility. Don't forget undergarments, a sports bra for activities, and comfortable sleepwear. Keep the microclimates in mind and pack accordingly. If you are planning to visit higher elevations and volcanoes, don't forget to pack warmer clothing.

Sun Protection and Beach Gear

Hawaii's direct sun means that you can't forego protective measures. Include a wide-brimmed sun hat, sunglasses, and a UV rash guard for water activities. Take along with you at least one bathing suit, water shoes for children, and a beach bag for convenience. Consider renting snorkel gear and prioritize reef-safe sunscreen due to local regulations.

Essential Travel Gadgets and Accessories

Opt for practicality with low-heeled sandals or tennis shoes for exploration. Bring a daypack for daily excursions, and consider collapsible options. A fanny pack provides convenience for quick access to valuables, and a waterproof phone case ensures device protection. Pack essentials like smartphones, charging cords, and earbuds.

Travel Documents and Copies

Make sure to keep all your travel essentials, such as IDs, plane tickets, reservations, itineraries, and any health-related travel requirements, in one easy-to-reach spot. Take a moment to assemble an emergency contact card for yourself as a traveler and create digital copies of your important documents. Be sure to understand the visa regulations and check if there are any specific health documents needed.

In today's world, it's wise to go digital with your travel paperwork as an extra precaution. Scan or take pictures of your passports, IDs, visas, tickets, and itineraries, and store them securely in digital formats. Consider using cloud services or encrypted USB drives for an additional layer of protection. This approach makes it easier to access crucial information swiftly, reducing the impact of losing physical documents. Create a concise and easily understandable emergency contact card containing:

- **Personal information:** Full name, date of birth, and blood type.

- **Emergency contacts:** Include at least two contacts with their relationship, phone numbers, and email addresses.

- **Medical information:** Any relevant medical conditions, allergies, or medications.

- **Travel insurance details:** Policy number, provider contact, and coverage details.

Section 3: Getting Around

When you're ready to discover the beautiful scenery of Oahu, it's important to know how to get around smoothly for a delightful experience. Let me give you a brief rundown of the main ways to get around: renting a car, using public transportation, or opting for rideshares.

Public Transportation

For a wallet-friendly and local vibe during your stay, why not hop on Oahu Transit Services, affectionately known as The Bus. Routes #19 and #20 cover the island, making it super convenient to reach all the must-see spots and neighborhoods. If you prefer a more personalized and private ride, you can easily find taxis and limousines too.

Rentals

When it comes to exploring Oahu on your own terms, renting a car is a popular choice. Well-known companies like Hertz, Avis, Enterprise, and Budget have setups at the Daniel K. Inouye International Airport and various spots around the island, ensuring a smooth pickup and drop-off experience. For an even wider array of choices, take a look at online travel agencies and booking platforms such as Expedia, Kayak, or Rentalcars.com. These platforms let you compare prices and find the perfect wheels for your Oahu adventure. Oahu offers a plethora of vacation rentals, apartments, and houses to suit every taste. However, if your main focus is securing a rental car, it's a good idea to stick with established car rental companies for reliability and a broader selection.

Navigating Oahu's Road System

Here are some tips to navigate Oahu's roads effectively:

Interstate highway system: Oahu's main roads are the H-1, H-2, and H-3. Take a moment to get acquainted with these highways and their connections; they basically serve as the island's road backbone. Knowing your way around these routes will make it easier to plan your trips and get to your destinations without a hitch.

Local maps and GPS: Equip yourself with a local map or use a GPS device to navigate Oahu's streets and highways. This is especially handy if you're not familiar with the area or if you find yourself stuck in traffic.

Stay alert and follow traffic rules: Oahu's streets can get pretty busy, so it's important to stay alert while driving. Make sure you follow traffic rules and keep an eye out for road signs to ensure a safe journey.

Construction projects: Stay in the loop about ongoing construction projects by checking updates from the Hawaii Department of Transportation. Being aware of road conditions and potential construction areas will help you plan your routes effectively and avoid unnecessary traffic delays.

Tips for Efficient and Budget-Friendly Travel in Oahu

Exploring Oahu on a budget? Fear not, as there are plenty of savvy ways to make the most of your trip without breaking the bank.

- **Utilize public transportation:** Oahu boasts an extensive and affordable public transportation system called The Bus. For just $2.75 (adults) or $1.25 (children) per one-way trip, and $5.50 (adults) or $2.50 (children) for a one-day pass, you can efficiently navigate the island without burning a hole in your pocket (Galea, n.d.).

- **Opt for budget-friendly accommodations:** Look beyond the main tourist areas for affordable lodging options. Consider vacation rentals, hostels, or hotels located outside the bustling tourist hubs. Home exchange programs can also provide a unique and budget-friendly accommodation experience.

- **Cook your own meals:** If your accommodation includes a kitchen, take advantage of it. Cooking your meals not only saves money but also allows you to savor local ingredients and flavors without dining out for every meal.

- **Shop at local markets:** Explore local swap meets and markets to find souvenirs and goods at more affordable prices compared to touristy shops. It's a great way to support local vendors and take home unique finds.

- **Enjoy free activities:** Embrace the wealth of free activities Oahu offers, from hiking and snorkeling to exploring local parks and beaches. Nature's beauty comes without a price tag, and these activities provide memorable experiences.

- **Leverage memberships:** If you have memberships to attractions like the Bishop Museum, take advantage of free admissions in Hawaii (Melissa, 2020).

Check if your existing memberships offer perks that can enhance your budget-friendly travel experience.

- **Hunt for flight specials:** Keep an eye out for flight specials, especially on Hawaiian Airlines. Look for deals, particularly if you're flying from the West Coast or JFK in New York.

- **Consider rental cars strategically:** Renting a car for specific days and relying on public transportation for the rest of your stay can be a cost-effective approach. Evaluate your itinerary and transportation needs to find the most budget-friendly solution.

Walking and Biking in Oahu

Oahu boasts several pedestrian-friendly areas, inviting you to explore charming neighborhoods on foot. Check out these walkable gems:

1. **Kaimuki:** An urban neighborhood that hosts a variety of popular Honolulu restaurants and shops.

2. **Chinatown district:** A vibrant crossroads near downtown Honolulu featuring groovy bars, eateries, art enclaves, stylish retailers, and multicultural businesses and markets.

3. **Kakaako:** This thriving urban center has become a popular destination thanks to redevelopment and the Pow Wow street mural and art movement.

4. **Kailua-Kona's Alii Drive:** A coastal road surrounded by restaurants offering island-fresh food, cafes with the scent of Kona coffee, tiny food carts, eclectic local boutiques, and a few galleries.

Bike Rental Options

1. **Viator:** Offers various bike rental options, including fat tire e-bikes and Hawaiian style e-bikes in Honolulu.

2. **Love Big Island:** Provides information on bike rental shops in Hilo, Kona, Waimea, and Waikoloa. Rental prices range from $25 for basic bikes to $100+ for premium options.

3. **Bike Hawaii:** Offers eBike tours, bicycle tours, hiking tours, and snorkel

tours in Honolulu, providing a range of outdoor adventure options.

4. **Paradise Baby Co:** Provides bike rentals and delivery services across the island, including the North Shore, Kailua, Ko'olina, and Hawaii Kai.

Scenic Trails

- **North Shore, Oahu:** Enjoy safe bike paths for scenic rides, exploring the coastline, and visiting various beaches. Recommended trails include the Magic Island loop, Pearl Harbor Bike Path, Ke Ala Pupukea, and Koko Head BMX track.

- **Turtle Bay Resort:** Features 12 miles of North Shore biking and hiking trails, allowing visitors to explore the resort's 850 acres of tropical paradise and secluded shoreline.

Whether you prefer a leisurely stroll or an adventurous bike ride, Oahu offers diverse experiences for every traveler.

Safety Considerations for Pedestrians and Cyclists in Oahu

When exploring Oahu on foot, it's crucial to prioritize safety. Here are key considerations:

- **Awareness and visibility:** Pedestrians should remain vigilant, never assuming that drivers see them, even when they have the right of way. Visibility is paramount for pedestrian safety. Resources like Walk Wise Hawaii provide valuable information on pedestrian safety.

- **Occupying bike lanes:** Pedestrians should avoid walking or jogging in bike lanes, as it poses safety concerns for both pedestrians and cyclists.

For those exploring Oahu on two wheels, adhering to safety guidelines is imperative:

- **Obeying traffic laws:** Cyclists must follow traffic laws, including stopping at stop signs and red lights. Riding with the flow of traffic and stopping at driveways enhances safety.

- **Helmet use:** Protecting against head injuries is paramount. Cyclists are advised to wear helmets consistently, regardless of the distance or speed of their ride.

- **Bike maintenance:** Before starting a cycling adventure, riders should ensure their bikes are in optimal condition. Regular checks of brakes, tires, and overall bike condition contribute to a safe riding experience.

- **Sharing the road:** Both motorists and cyclists share the responsibility of road safety. Motorists should provide a minimum of 3 feet of space when passing cyclists, while cyclists should ride predictably, avoiding actions that may surprise drivers.

Understanding and adhering to regulations is essential for a safe journey. In Waikiki, riding bicycles, skateboards, or roller skates on sidewalks is prohibited. Familiarize yourself with local regulations regarding cycling and pedestrian activities to ensure a safe and enjoyable experience.

Section 4: Weather

Oahu boasts a unique climate characterized by mild temperatures, moderate humidity, and persistent northeasterly trade winds. Seasonal variations shape the weather patterns, categorizing the year into two main seasons: "summer" from May to October and "winter" from October to April.

Offshore storms in the Pacific Ocean can bring strong winds, creating high surf conditions along different shorelines. Tropical cyclones pose a significant threat, producing storm surges and large waves, with the potential to reach heights over 20 feet. As hurricane season spans from June 1 to November 30, beachgoers are advised to stay informed through local weather reports for any active threats.

Understanding emergency preparedness and staying alert to local advisories ensures safety during varying weather conditions. As weather conditions can change rapidly, it is crucial to be well-informed and adhere to recommended safety measures.

Section 5: Geography

Oahu's geographical diversity offers an array of landscapes to explore, each region presenting unique highlights and attractions.

From the vibrant city life of Honolulu to the lush beauty of the Windward Coast, Oahu's regions showcase distinct characteristics. The North Shore boasts world-renowned surf spots, while the Central Oahu plains offer historical sites and agricultural landscapes.

Honolulu, the capital, combines urban sophistication with cultural richness. The Windward Coast captivates with its scenic beauty, encompassing lush valleys and pristine beaches. The Leeward Coast offers a more laid-back atmosphere, while the North Shore is a haven for surf enthusiasts. Central Oahu provides a glimpse into the island's history and agricultural heritage.

Each geographic area hosts popular attractions and activities, such as the historic Pearl Harbor in Honolulu, the iconic Waimea Bay on the North Shore, and the scenic Byodo-In Temple on the Windward Coast. Visitors can immerse themselves in diverse landscapes, ensuring a well-rounded Oahu experience.

Section 6: Traveling With Children

Oahu welcomes families with an abundance of kid-friendly attractions and experiences. From the interactive exhibits at the Honolulu Children's Discovery Center to the mesmerizing marine life at the Waikiki Aquarium, the island offers a plethora of engaging activities for children.

Prioritizing safety is essential when traveling with children. Families should be mindful of ocean safety, adhere to beach guidelines, and ensure children are equipped with appropriate sun protection. Additionally, it's advisable to have a family emergency plan and be aware of healthcare facilities on the island.

For added convenience, Oahu provides childcare services and facilities, allowing parents to enjoy some adult time or explore attractions that may not be suitable for younger children. Resorts often offer kids' clubs, and reputable childcare providers cater to families seeking reliable assistance during their stay.

Section 7: The People

Aloha, beyond a greeting or farewell, embodies love, peace, compassion, and mutual respect. It signifies living harmoniously with the land and its people, embracing mercy, sympathy, grace, and kindness. Greeting someone with aloha fosters mutual regard and affection.

Upon arrival, experiencing a lei, a floral garland symbolizing friendship and welcome, is customary. It's considered rude to remove it in public. Regular use of words like "aloha" (hello, goodbye, love) and "mahalo" (thank you) is encouraged. Kindness is paramount—hold doors open, express gratitude, and be courteous.

Hula, more than entertainment, is a sacred dance rooted in Hawaiian tradition. Watching hula performances is common, but it's crucial to respect its cultural significance. Mocking or joining in without invitation disregards the art's dedication and sacred storytelling.

Removing shoes before entering homes is a sign of respect. This tradition, influenced by Japanese customs, prevents bringing dirt indoors, maintaining cleanliness, and showing consideration for the hosts.

Preserving Hawaii's pristine beaches is vital. Smoking is often prohibited, and disposing of cigarette butts in the sand harms marine life. Abide by local laws and use designated areas for smoking, emphasizing responsible tourism.

Show respect for sacred sites and traditions, engage in sustainable tourism practices, and participate in cultural events with reverence. Cultivate cultural awareness to enhance your experience and contribute positively to the local community.

Section 8: Hawaiian Time and Shaka

"Hawaiian Time" encapsulates the unhurried, laid-back approach to life in Hawaii. Locals prioritize enjoying the present, fostering a unique rhythm that may differ from mainland expectations.

Visitors should align with local schedules, allowing for a more immersive experience. Patience and flexibility are key when adapting to the relaxed pace, ensuring a harmonious blend of relaxation and planned activities.

Harmonizing leisure with scheduled endeavors enhances the Hawaiian experience. Embrace spontaneity, savoring moments of tranquility amidst planned adventures.

The Shaka sign, a thumb and pinkie gesture, has diverse origin stories. One credits Hamana Kalili's sugar mill accident, while others link it to Spanish immigrants or visiting whalers. The late Lippy Espinda's influence on its popularity is notable, although debates surround his claim as the originator (The Origin of the Hawaiian "Shaka," 2019).

Understanding the Shaka's versatile meanings—from greeting and gratitude to expressing approval—ensures respectful use in diverse situations.

Incorporating the Shaka into interactions and embracing the island's relaxed vibe enhances cultural immersion. Visitors adopting the Shaka contribute positively to the spirit of aloha, fostering a connection with the local community.

Section 9: Hawaiian Language

- **Aloha–Hello (Pronounced a-lo-ha)**

  - Meaning more than a simple greeting, "Aloha" embodies love, kindness, compassion, and peace. Used for various greetings, it wishes a positive and respectful life.

- **Mahalo–Thank you (Pronounced mah-hah-loh)**

  - Express gratitude with "Mahalo." The phrase reflects a culture of admiration and respect, evolving from a deeply grateful Hawaiian society.

- **'A' ole Pilikia–You're welcome/No problem (Pronounced ah-oh-leh pee-lee-kee-yah)**

  - Embracing Hawaii's community-driven culture, this response to "Mahalo" emphasizes a shared sense of gratitude.

- **A Hui Hou–Until we meet again (Pronounced ah-hoo-wee-ho-oo-uu)**

  - Similar to "see you soon," often heard at lū'au concerts in place of "encore."

- **Howzit?–How are you? (Pronounced how-zit)**

- A casual greeting meaning "what's up?" akin to the South African usage. Often paired with "braddah" for brother.

Section 10: Music

Hawaiian music, deeply rooted in a rich thousand-year-old heritage, echoes with the spirit of traditional rhythms, chants, and vocal expressions. Hawaiian music in the 19th century evolved into the wide range of styles we hear today as a result of various factors, including early missionaries' hymns. From rock 'n roll and rap to jazz and Jawaiian (Hawaiian reggae), the music vividly reflects the cultural blend found in the islands. Festivals like the 'Ukulele Festival in July pay tribute to the instrument's history, introduced to Hawaii by Portuguese immigrants. Similarly, the Kona Slack Key Festival in September honors the unique local slack key guitar style, capturing the breezy, flowing essence of Hawaiian climate and culture.

Section 11: Farmer's Market

Discover the rich farm-to-table experience in Hawaii, where travelers are warmly invited to delve into the diverse offerings at farmers' markets and fruit stands scattered across the islands. These vibrant markets not only showcase a colorful array of fruits and flowers but also feature local delights such as Hawai'i-grown coffee, flavorful jams, crunchy macadamia nuts, and delectable treats from renowned restaurants.

Maui, in particular, is celebrated for its renowned markets offering huli huli chicken, luscious papayas, and creamy avocados. Meanwhile, the Hāna Farms, nestled along the scenic Hāna Highway, beckon with refreshing juices. Over on Kaua'i, the "Sunshine Markets" flourish, and O'ahu's KCC Farmers Market stands as a major attraction.

From the fertile volcanic soils of Hawai'i island to the serene landscapes of Lāna'i and Moloka'i, each market unveils unique treasures that turn every stop into a delightful culinary adventure.

Segue: In this chapter, we've talked at length about the diverse landscapes of Oahu, delving into its transportation options, road systems, budget-friendly travel tips, and pedestrian-friendly areas. We've embraced the Aloha spirit, understanding its cultural significance and essential etiquettes. Hawaiian time and the Shaka sign have been unveiled, offering insights into the island's laid-back vibe. Additionally, we've explored the richness of the Hawaiian language, with essential phrases to enhance your cultural experience. From music festivals to farmer's markets, we've unveiled the heart and soul of Oahu's local life. Now, get ready for the next leg of your journey as we prepare ourselves for the adventure of hiking to the iconic Diamond Head Summit, promising breathtaking views and an immersive experience in Oahu's natural wonders.

Chapter Two

Diamond Head

A'ohe hana nui ke alu 'ia," or "No task is too great when undertaken together."

T his Hawaiian proverb beautifully encapsulates the spirit of our journey as we dive into Chapter 2. As we embark on this adventure, envision yourself not just as a traveler but as a part of a collective exploration. Our aim is to make planning your hike up the Diamond Head Summit a breeze.

Diamond Head, or Lēʻahi in Hawaiian, emerges as a volcanic cone on Oʻahu Island, Hawaii, renowned for its historical and geological significance. The name, a fusion of Hawaiian terms, lae (brow-ridge) and ʻahi (tuna), alludes to the ridge-line's resemblance to a tuna's dorsal fin. Initially dubbed Diamond Hill by British sailors in 1825, owing to the discovery of calcite crystals on its shores, the moniker endures (Dimple, 2023).

Belonging to the Honolulu Volcanic Series, alongside other notable O'ahu landmarks, Diamond Head boasts an age estimated at around 300,000 years. Throughout history, this site and its environs played a pivotal role in military strategy, hosting Fort Ruger, Hawaii's inaugural U.S. military reservation. Presently, remnants like Battery 407 and the Birkhimer Tunnel within the crater stand as historical artifacts, serving as a testament to Diamond Head's military legacy (Dimple, 2023). As visitors ascend its slopes, they set off not only on a geological journey but also step back in time, tracing the imprints of military history that echo through the ages. So, fasten your seatbelts, or should I say, lace up those hiking boots as we unfold the secrets, tips, and joyous moments that await you on this thrilling ascent!

Reservations for out-of-state visitors is required and can easily be done on their website. This can be done 30 days in advance. The time is scheduled in 2-hour blocks, and you must arrive within 30 minutes of your assigned block to gain entry.

Hiking Essentials

Undertaking the Diamond Head hike promises a remarkable adventure, and to ensure you make the most of it, proper preparation is key. Here's a checklist of hiking essentials to make your journey up the iconic summit not only enjoyable but safe:

- **Sturdy footwear:** Lace up those reliable hiking boots or athletic shoes with good traction. The trail presents varying terrains, and solid footwear will provide the necessary grip and support.

- **Hydration:** Bring a refillable water bottle to stay hydrated throughout the hike. The Hawaiian sun can be intense, and proper hydration is crucial for an energized and enjoyable experience.

- **Sun protection:** Don't underestimate the Hawaiian sun. Pack sunscreen with a high SPF, sunglasses to shield your eyes, and a hat for extra protection. Consider lightweight, long-sleeved clothing to cover exposed skin.

- **Snacks:** Energize yourself with light snacks like energy bars or trail mix. Keeping your energy levels up ensures you have the stamina to conquer the ascent.

- **Backpack:** Carry a small backpack to store your essentials. It will keep your hands free, allowing you to navigate the trail comfortably.

- **Weather-appropriate clothing:** Check the weather forecast and dress accordingly. A light jacket or rain poncho might come in handy if the weather takes an unexpected turn.

- **Camera/Smartphone:** Capture the breathtaking views from the summit. Whether it's a camera or your smartphone, having a device to document your achievement is a must.

- **Trail map:** While the Diamond Head trail is well-marked, having a trail map can be beneficial, especially if you plan on exploring side trails.

Preparing for the Diamond Head hike involves tailoring your approach to the trail's moderate difficulty, accommodating varying fitness levels. Regardless of your fitness level, start with regular walks or light exercises to build stamina. Gradually increase the intensity to ensure you're ready for the ascent. Focus on cardiovascular exercises to enhance endurance, crucial for the climb.

Navigating the trail demands attention to designated paths. Stay on marked trails to preserve the delicate ecosystem and prevent erosion. Diamond Head's summit offers breathtaking views, and respecting the designated routes ensures the sustainability of this natural beauty.

As you ascend, pace yourself. Take breaks when needed, especially in shaded areas along the trail. The journey is as important as the destination, allowing you to appreciate the diverse flora and unique geological features.

Aim to start your hike early to avoid the midday heat, and always check the weather forecast. Hawaii's weather can change, so be prepared for sun or rain. By combining physical readiness with trail awareness, you'll maximize the enjoyment of your Diamond Head hike while maintaining the beauty of this natural wonder.

About the Hike

- **Trail length:** The trail to the summit is 0.8 mile (1.3 km) one way, offering a manageable yet engaging hike.

- **Trail head:** Located adjacent to the parking lot within Diamond Head State Monument, the entrance is off Diamond Head Road between Makapu'u Avenue and 18th Avenue, Honolulu.

- **Time:** Depending on your pace and how much you savor the scenic spots, the hike can take around 1 to 1.5 hours.

- **Activity:** The trail is a captivating blend of nature and history, providing insights into the geological and military significance of Diamond Head Crater. You'll encounter a mix of natural tuff surfaces, switchbacks, stairs, and even a lighted tunnel.

- **Difficulty:** Moderately challenging with uneven and steep sections, including stairways. Take your time and wear appropriate footwear.

- **Terrain:** Much of the trail traverses the steep interior slope of the crater wall, offering diverse landscapes and geological features.

- **Elevation gain:** Climbing 560 feet (171 m) in elevation, the ascent presents a satisfying challenge without being overly strenuous.

- **Trail brochure:** For a detailed guide, refer to the official trail brochure here.

- Info: Additional

  - *Mountain biking:* Not allowed on this trail.

  - *Stay on the trail:* Preserve the natural environment by sticking to designated paths.

  - *No dogs:* Pets are not allowed in Diamond Head State Monument.

  - *Pack out:* Adhere to the "leave no trace" principle by taking out at least what you brought in.

  - *No open fires:* Help maintain the ecological balance by refraining from open fires.

  - *Hiking permit:* Not required for groups less than 25.

- **Facilities:** Limited facilities are available, so it's advisable to bring essentials like water and snacks.

- **Hazards:** Be cautious on uneven terrain and steep sections. Use appropriate footwear and take your time navigating through stairs and the lighted tunnel.

- **Prohibited:** Mountain biking, dogs, and open fires are prohibited to preserve the natural environment and ensure a safe hiking experience.

From the initial paved walkway to the summit's stunning panorama, every step is a glimpse into the vibrant history of this volcanic crater.

Reaching Diamond Head Hike from Waikiki Beach

The Diamond Head hike is truly an adventure, and the journey to the trailhead can be just as delightful. You've got a couple of options to get there:

If you fancy a stroll: Take a leisurely walk from Waikiki to Diamond Head, covering roughly 3 miles. It's a charming journey lasting around an hour to an hour and a half, depending on your pace. Start your walk at the picturesque Fort Derussy Beach Park, setting the scene for a scenic adventure. As you follow the coastal walkway, be prepared for a treat as stunning views unfolding along the way, with a residential area graced by tropical flowers and swaying palm trees.

If you prefer a hassle-free ride: Opt for the bus. It is a convenient choice to get from Waikiki to the Diamond Head State Monument stop. The duration of the bus ride clocks in at about 15 to 20 minutes, offering a hassle-free transit option, traffic-dependent, of course. Whether you choose the leisurely stroll or the bus ride, each option is a step closer to the exciting trails of Diamond Head, promising a journey as captivating as the destination itself.

Walking and Bus

Some visitors prefer to walk to Diamond Head from Waikiki and then take the bus back. This way, you can relish the scenic surroundings on your way to the hike and conveniently avoid walking back after completing the trail.

Diamond Head is just 3 miles from Waikiki, and driving takes around 15 to 20 minutes, depending on traffic. However, parking is limited and comes at a fee of $10 per car. If you choose to drive, consider starting your hike early in the day (Fitzsimons, 2023).

For a hassle-free public transport option, take the Waikiki Trolley. While it's pricier than the bus, starting at $25 for a one-day ticket for adults, it's a convenient hop-on-hop-off system with easy access points in Waikiki (Fitzsimons, 2023).

Whether you prefer a leisurely walk, a budget-friendly bus ride, or the convenience of a trolley, getting to the Diamond Head hike from Waikiki is an integral part of the overall experience. Choose the option that aligns with your preferences, and get ready for an unforgettable adventure.

What to Expect Upon Arrival on the Hike

A bit of foresight on this hike goes a long way. Here's what you should keep in mind upon reaching your destination:

Be ready to part with $10 per vehicle if you choose to park at the site. Alternatively, for those bypassing the crater parking, the fee stands at $5 per person, whether you walk in or arrive by bus, taxi, trolley, or rideshare.

Brace yourself for a demanding hike through steep, exposed terrain with no respite from the sun. Equip yourself with good walking shoes, a hat, sunglasses, sunscreen, and, most importantly, sufficient water. The 1.6-mile roundtrip hike boasts a 560-foot elevation gain, making it particularly strenuous, especially on hotter days. Expect crowds, especially between 8 a.m. and 4 p.m., as this sought-after tourist spot attracts a steady stream of visitors during these hours. To savor a less bustling experience, plan your visit either in the early hours before 8 a.m. or later in the day. If navigating traffic and parking stresses you out, you might want to consider public transport options like the bus, trolley, or rideshare for a smoother journey.

The hike offers multiple lookout points along the trail. Expect a wait at popular vantage spots as everyone endeavors to capture the stunning views.

Brace yourself for a challenging ascent, but rest assured, the reward is worth it. The panoramic views of the terrain, ocean, and Waikiki beaches await at the summit.

Upon reaching the Diamond Head Crater, be mindful of the entry fees for out-of-state visitors. Whether you conquer the trail's elevation gain or rest at the lookout points, the hike offers a mix of physical challenge and breathtaking scenery. Don't forget your essentials, arrive strategically to beat the crowds, and get ready for an adventure that balances effort with the awe-inspiring beauty of Diamond Head.

Cost of Diamond Head Hike

The Diamond Head hike comes with a few costs to consider. If you call Hawaii home, you're in for a treat because no entry fee for you! Hawaii residents enjoy complimentary access, making it a lucky perk. However, for those of us not fortunate enough to reside in the beautiful state, the entry fee stands at $5 per person, while the little ones under 3 get a free pass. When it's time to settle the entry fee, remember to reach for your trusty credit card; they only accept plastic, so cash won't do the trick.

Now, let's talk parking. Hawaii residents, you've got it good since parking is on the house for you. But for non-residents cruising in with their non-commercial vehicles, it's a $10 ticket to park. If you're rolling in with a commercial vehicle, be prepared for fees ranging from $25 to $90. A friendly reminder: just like the entry fee, parking fees are strictly credit card transactions. So, make sure that plastic is ready to roll; cash won't secure your parking spot. It's the little details that make the journey smooth, so be equipped and enjoy your adventure at Diamond Head.

Panoramic Views and Photo Ops

Prepare for a visual feast as you conquer the Diamond Head summit. The breathtaking panorama awaits, showcasing the beauty of Waikiki, Honolulu, and the vast Pacific Ocean. Here's what to expect and how to capture those Instagram-worthy shots:

Once you reach the summit, let the beauty unfold. Behold the 360-degree views that stretch from Koko Head to Kaena Point. Take in the stunning sights of Honolulu Harbor, Waikiki Beach, and the endless expanse of the Pacific Ocean.

Explore the vantage points and discover the historical remnants, including World War II-era bunkers that add a touch of intrigue to the scenic landscape.

Best Times for Photography

- Set your alarm early for a sunrise hike. The morning light casts a golden glow over Waikiki and Honolulu, creating a magical atmosphere. Capture the sun's first rays illuminating the landscape for an unforgettable photo.

- Alternatively, plan an evening hike for a sunset spectacle. The changing hues of the sky, coupled with the city lights coming to life, paint a serene backdrop for your snapshots.

Iconic Diamond Head Crater

- Don't miss the chance to photograph the iconic Diamond Head crater itself. The geological marvel, with its distinct shape and volcanic history, is a centerpiece of your visual adventure.

- Explore the eight lookout points along the crater rim for different angles and perspectives. Each offers a unique frame for your photos.

Capturing the Essence

- The trail itself provides numerous opportunities for action shots. Capture fellow hikers conquering the trail, especially during moments of triumph as they reach the summit.

- Visit the historic lighthouse and museum. Document the artifacts and immerse yourself in the rich history of Diamond Head. Share snapshots of 19th-century navigational tools and captivating exhibits.

Tips for the Perfect Shot

- Arrive early in the morning or late afternoon for favorable lighting conditions and fewer crowds.

- Given the popularity of the hike, be patient during peak hours. Consider arriving before 8 a.m. or exploring later in the day to avoid midday crowds.

So, charge your camera, pack your enthusiasm, and get ready to capture the essence of Diamond Head.

Segue: In wrapping up our exploration of conquering the iconic Diamond Head Summit, we've unveiled the secrets to a seamless hike, ensuring your journey to this geological gem is not just memorable but perfectly planned. From essential hiking gear to navigating the trail with ease, you're now armed with insights to make your Diamond Head experience truly extraordinary.

As we bid aloha to Diamond Head, we're not just closing one chapter; we're opening the door to another exciting adventure—the beautiful trek to Manoa Falls. Picture yourself amidst lush rainforests, the soothing sounds of cascading water guiding your way. But before we set foot on this verdant trail, let's reflect on the takeaways from our Diamond Head journey. Embrace the panoramic views, cherish the historical echoes, and relish the sense of accomplishment as you stand atop this ancient volcanic cone.

Now, fasten your laces and grab that water bottle because, in the upcoming chapter, we're looking into the secrets of hiking to Manoa Falls. From the enchanting trailhead to the captivating cascade awaiting you at the end, get ready to immerse yourself in the allure of Oahu's natural wonders. So, adventurers, take your backpacks and get ready for a journey into the heart of a rainforest, where the magic of Manoa Falls beckons. It's not just a hike; it's an exploration of the island's captivating landscapes and the allure of a pristine waterfall oasis. The trail awaits, so let's dive into the next chapter and unlock the secrets of Manoa Falls!

Chapter Three

Manoa Falls

To my mind, the greatest reward and luxury of travel is to be able to experience everyday things as if for the first time. —Bill Bryson

These words from Bill Bryson really hit home, especially when you're gearing up for a trip to witness the stunning Manoa Falls in Oahu. Imagine standing in front of a breathtaking waterfall, plunging 150 feet down the mountainside, a view so captivating that it will remain etched in your memory forever. In fact, it'll make you feel like you're gazing at a waterfall ten times its actual height. And there's some good news for you, too. The hike to this magnificent beauty has recently improved, with some upgrades that make the journey more enjoyable and, to some extent, better. Believe me, I've hiked this trail both before and after the improvements, and the difference is remarkable. The path is now smoother, easier to follow, and provides an even more immersive experience in the lush beauty of Oahu's landscape. So, if you're up for an adventure filled with natural marvels and breathtaking scenery, come along as we explore all the details you need to plan the perfect hike to Manoa Falls.

Trail Details: What to Expect

Choosing the trail to Manoa Falls is an adventure that promises to be as rewarding as the destination itself. It's not only famous among the tourists but locals too. Nestled at the end of Manoa Road, approximately 2 miles above the University of Hawaii, the trailhead is like a hidden gem waiting to be discovered. Getting there is part of the journey, and it's accessible by various means, from driving to catching a bus.

Now, let's talk about the trail itself. Considered moderately challenging, it caters to a range of fitness levels, making it an ideal choice for both seasoned hikers and those seeking a moderate adventure. It's definitely not a walk in the park, but at the same time, it's not too tough. Covering a round-trip distance of about 1.6 miles (2.6 km), the trail offers a perfect balance of exploration without being overwhelmingly long. As you tread along, the trail gently goes uphill, providing just enough challenge to keep things interesting without being too demanding.

No adventure would be complete without considering permits and regulations. The good news is, hiking Manoa Falls doesn't require any permits. It's a liberating feeling to know you can go on this journey without bureaucratic hurdles. Yet, as responsible hikers, respecting posted regulations and guidelines is crucial. It ensures the sustainability of the trail and the preservation of the natural beauty that makes this hike so special.

Navigation is a key aspect of any successful hike. While the trail isn't a maze, having a map is like having a trustworthy companion on your journey. Get familiar with the trailhead location, and consider using trail guides or online resources for that extra layer of navigation help. It'll point you in the right direction, making sure you don't miss any of the trail's hidden gems.

The trail beckons with promises of natural beauty, a moderate challenge, and the joy of discovering a waterfall that will leave you awestruck.

Now, let's talk about the gear and equipment that will ensure you're well-prepared for the trail of Manoa Falls. First things first, your footwear. Slip into sturdy hiking shoes or boots with reliable traction.

Dress the part with lightweight, quick-drying clothing made from moisture-wicking materials. It will protect you against the elements, providing comfort as you traverse the trail. The Hawaiian sun can be quite intense, so don't forget your sunscreen, hat, and sunglasses—your shield against the sun's harsh rays. Tuck away a non-toxic insect repellent in your bag to keep those pesky bugs at bay.

Hydration is key, so bring along plenty of water in a reusable bottle. It will keep you refreshed throughout the hike while also reducing single-use plastic waste. As you navigate the sometimes muddy and slippery trail, opt for sneakers with a good grip or sturdy hiking boots. A light rain jacket is a wise addition to your gear, especially in Manoa Falls' rainforest setting.

Now, let's talk about packing. Consider one like the Patagonia Women's Nine Trails Pack 18L—comfortable and spacious enough for your adventure necessities. Don't forget a basic first aid kit, a whistle, and a flashlight—safety essentials recommended by the Department of Land and Natural Resources (DLNR). And, of course, your camera—because who wouldn't want to capture the breathtaking views of Manoa Falls?

Safety is paramount, so take note of some precautions.

While the allure of taking a refreshing dip in the waterfall might be tempting, it's a strict no-no for a crucial reason. The water flowing from Manoa Falls carries Leptospirosis, a disease that can lead to mild to moderate flu-like symptoms persisting for 1 to 2 weeks (Complete Guide to the Manoa Falls Hike Oahu Adventure, 2023). Trust me; it's not the kind of memory you'd want as a keepsake from your Oahu trip.

And that's not the only cautionary note for your Manoa Falls adventure. Keep your wits about you to avoid unexpected surprises on the trail. Falling rocks, especially near the waterfall, can pose a risk. Stay vigilant and heed cautionary signs to prevent any impromptu rock showers that might dampen your hike.

Navigating the trails can be a slippery slope, quite literally. The tropical weather can transform paths into muddy stretches. Ensure you've got the right footwear with a good grip to maneuver these potentially treacherous terrains safely.

Timing is everything, and here's the lowdown for your Manoa Falls hike. The trail is approximately 1.6 miles roundtrip, taking about 1-2 hours to complete. Arriving early or later in the day is your secret weapon against crowds and unpredictable weather. And speaking of weather, plan to finish your hike well before sunset. Picture yourself basking in the glow of accomplishment as the sun dips below the horizon.

Now, let's talk about getting yourself physically prepared for the adventure that awaits you at Manoa Falls. While the trail is relatively flat, it can get rocky and slippery, especially after a bout of rain. Ensuring you're in good physical condition and sporting appropriate footwear can be a game-changer, helping prevent any accidents or injuries along the way.

First things first, let's gauge your fitness level. Take a moment to assess whether the trail aligns with your abilities. It's always better to go on a journey that suits your physical capabilities, ensuring a more enjoyable experience without any unnecessary strain.

Before you hit the trail, indulge in some light stretching to warm up those muscles. It's like giving your body a gentle wake-up call, priming it for the adventure ahead. Stretching not only helps prevent injuries but also enhances your flexibility, making navigating the terrain a breeze.

It's time we talk about parking and cost logistics. At the Paradise Park parking lot, conveniently located at the trailhead, you'll find designated parking areas. For non-residents, the parking fee is a reasonable $7 per car, while residents enjoy a discounted rate of $4. Alternatively, if you're up for a little stroll, you can opt for free parking in the nearby residential neighborhood before the park entrance and take a leisurely half-mile walk to the park. Keep in mind that the parking lot operates from 8 am to 6 pm daily, so plan your arrival accordingly (Manoa Falls Hike: Trail Guide and Useful Hiking Tips, 2023).

Here are some additional tips for you:

- As you gear up for your hike, remember that the trail can often be muddy and slippery. That's where sturdy hiking shoes come into play, offering the traction you need to navigate through the lush wilderness with ease. Consider bringing along a change of shoes if you plan to explore other destinations post-hike, ensuring your feet stay dry and comfortable throughout your adventures.

- To witness the waterfall in all its majestic glory, consider embarking on your hike shortly after rainfall. The cascade will be stronger and fuller, painting a picture-perfect scene amidst the verdant backdrop of the rainforest. However, always remember to respect local guidelines and heed signs indicating when it's safe to proceed, ensuring a memorable and safe exploration of this natural wonder.

How to Reach Manoa Falls From Waikiki Beach

Getting to Manoa Falls from the vibrant Waikiki Beach is a breeze, offering you various transportation options to suit your preferences. So, let's break it down, making your journey as straightforward as a Hawaiian breeze.

By Car

If going by car suits you best, reaching Manoa Valley from Waikiki is a quick 15-minute drive. Simply hop onto the H-1 west, heading towards the airport, until you hit the Punahou exit. Follow Punahou Road, seamlessly transforming into Manoa Road, leading you straight to the trail's starting point. A designated parking lot awaits at the top of Manoa Road, requiring a modest $5 fee (Pauly, 2023). Yet, some hikers opt for the nearby residential area, offering free parking and just a short additional stroll.

By Bus

For those of you relying on public transport, route 5 of TheBus departing from Ala Moana Shopping Center is your go-to. A mere 10-minute walk from the bus stop lands you at the trailhead (Shaka Guide, n.d.). But here's the thing: getting to Manoa Falls by bus usually means you'll have to transfer. Since Manoa is more of a residential area, there aren't as many bus routes going through, so you'll need to plan for that extra part of the journey. Even though it's pretty close to the lively hub of Waikiki, navigating the neighborhood requires a bit of factoring in the transit aspect.

Expect to spend around 30 minutes on the bus, factoring in potential transfers based on your starting point in Waikiki. It's a laid-back ride, letting you soak in the scenery before your waterfall adventure.

Shuttle Services

Now, if you're seeking convenience coupled with a guided touch, shuttle services are at your beck and call. These convenient shuttles sweep through Waikiki hotels, whisking you away to the enchanting Manoa Falls. Beyond just transportation, you'll relish the added benefit of a guided tour, enhancing your journey with insights and stories. It's a hassle-free option, especially if you prefer a seamless travel experience without the fuss of coordinating different modes of transport (Shaka Guide, n.d.).

Whether you're behind the wheel, embracing the local bus experience, or opting for the guided ease of a shuttle, your route to Manoa Falls sets the stage for an adventure that begins the moment you decide to chase waterfalls in this Hawaiian paradise.

Picture and Photo Op at Manoa Falls

Going on the Manoa Falls trail isn't just a hike; it's a visual feast of Mother Nature's most splendid creations. You're surrounded by lush greenery, the air is alive with the sounds of a vibrant tropical forest.

The journey begins with the embrace of lush tropical forests, where each step immerses you deeper into nature's vibrant palette. Beautiful trees and vibrant foliage create a mesmerizing backdrop, a balance of green that spreads along the trail.

Then, the trail unveils its pièce de résistance—Manoa Falls, a majestic cascade standing tall at 100–150 feet. The views are nothing short of stunning, beckoning every photographer's lens to capture the sheer beauty of this natural spectacle.

Your camera will be your best companion as you navigate the trail, offering opportunities to capture the waterfall from various angles. Standing at the bottom of the falls, a small pool forming beneath, framing the cascade in a perfect frame of water and rocks, is an experience of a lifetime.

Along the trail, a unique feature awaits—a tree arch that not only offers a mesmerizing perspective but also stands as a great photo opportunity.

For those seeking a more secluded experience, the hike to the upper portion of Manoa Falls is a must. Here, a beautiful infinity pool-like effect awaits, offering tranquility away from the bustling crowds.

From the upper reaches of the falls, your lens can capture breathtaking views of Manoa Valley. The scenery unfolds, stretching all the way to Waikiki, creating a visual masterpiece that reflects the true essence of this Hawaiian haven.

While swimming is strictly prohibited, the pool at the bottom of the lower falls tempts some visitors. Despite the prohibition, the allure of the water is undeniable, inviting an occasional rebel to dip their toes and seize a moment amidst the beauty.

And if you find yourself experiencing déjà vu amidst this natural wonderland, there's a reason. Scenes from the iconic "Jurassic Park" were filmed here, weaving the allure of Hollywood magic into the fabric of the hike. More recently, the lush rainforest set the stage for the TV series "Lost," leaving echoes of cinematic charm along the trail.

As you tread the opening stretch of the Manoa Falls Trail, crossing a quaint bridge, the surroundings transform into a wild haven. Vines drape the trees, and the forest reveals its untamed beauty. The trail passes alongside a stream, unveiling a diverse array of plant species, a living exhibit that begs you to pause and take a closer look.

So, grab your camera, lace up those hiking shoes, and get ready for a visual adventure along the Manoa Falls trail, where every turn is a frame-worthy masterpiece waiting to be captured.

Segue: In our journey through the lush wonders of Oahu, the Manoa Falls trail has unveiled itself as a true gem. As we saw the enchanting landscapes, the vibrant tropical forests, and the majestic cascade of Manoa Falls, we've captured moments that will linger in our memories. Manoa, shaped by the forces of a volcanic eruption and sculpted by rain, wind, and river, stands as a testament to nature's artistry. The early Hawaiians aptly named it Manoa, signifying its wide and vast expanse, a title that resonates with the deep valley and saw-tooth mountain ridges we've come to witness.

But our adventure doesn't end here. As we bid farewell to Manoa, we turn our gaze towards the Pillbox hike, the next chapter in our exploration. This captivating journey promises not just panoramic views but also a glimpse into the historical significance of the pillboxes that dot the landscape. What tales do these remnants of the past hold, and what vistas await us at the summit? Join me as we learn more about the Pillbox hike, where every step is a stride through history, and every ascent unveils a breathtaking panorama. The allure of Oahu's landscapes continues, beckoning us to look deeper into its wonders

Chapter Four

Pink Pill Box Hike

I travel not to go anywhere, but to go. I travel for travel's sake. The great affair is to move. —Robert Louis Stevenson

G etting ready for the next leg of our adventure, we find ourselves drawn to the enchanting Kaiwa Ridge Trail, affectionately known as the Pillbox Hike. As we lace up our hiking boots, we're not merely traversing landscapes; we're embracing the essence of exploration, the sheer joy of movement.

The Kaiwa Ridge Trail, woven into the rich tapestry of Oahu's history, unveils a chapter shaped by the echoes of World War II. Built as a strategic alternative route during wartime, the trail now stands as a testament to resilience and adaptability. Two weathered pillboxes, standing sentinel along the ridge, evoke stories of the past. Commissioned as Coast Artillery Observation Stations, these bunkers were not armed fortifications but served as lookout points, offering a 360-degree panorama of the coastal splendor (Dillingham, 2023).

Venturing into the Kaiwa Ridge Trail is not just a hike; it's a journey through time, a chance to walk in the footsteps of history. As we ascend, we'll encounter these concrete relics adorned with vibrant graffiti, a testament to the trail's evolving identity. The trail's charm lies not just in the physical exertion but in the tales it whispers through the coastal winds.

Ever wondered what the Lanikai Pillboxes were used for during the war? Well, not as armories or bunkers, but as vantage points that guarded the coast, watching over Oahu's shores. Today, they stand as witnesses to a bygone era, inviting hikers to climb down their ladders and immerse themselves in history.

And how many pillboxes await us at the summit? Two, standing about 400 feet apart, etched into the mountain's embrace (Dillingham, 2023). Their unique construction, embedded into the slope rather than perched on top, adds an element of intrigue. Visitors, often content with the breathtaking coastal views from above, can witness these relics of the past adorned with a splash of contemporary art.

So, fellow explorers, join me as we step into the Kaiwa Ridge Trail, where each stride echoes with tales of wartime ingenuity, resilience, and the timeless allure of the Hawaiian coastline. This chapter promises not just a hike but a walk through history, a chance to marvel at the convergence of the old and the new on Oahu's picturesque

landscapes. Let the Pillbox Hike unfold its stories as we traverse its slopes and ascend to new heights.

Things to Do: What to Expect

Imagine yourself hiking the Kaiwa Ridge Trail while admiring the verdant scenery all around you and listening to the soft whispers of the coastal breeze. The actual hiking part of the hike is pretty easy going, which means that you will be able to maintain a comfortable pace as you soak in the mesmerizing scenery. With each step, you'll find yourself effortlessly moving forward, drawn deeper into the enchanting landscape.

However, don't let the tranquility fool you; there will be certain challenging moments spread out evenly throughout the hike. Be prepared for several steep climbs that may temporarily slow your stride. These inclines, though demanding, add a touch of adventure to your journey, inviting you to conquer them with determination and perseverance. So, as you traverse the Pillbox Hike, embrace the ebb and flow of the terrain, knowing that each ascent and descent contributes to the tapestry of your hiking experience. In this section, you will find every piece of information necessary to complete this hike.

Trail Information

Now, let's delve into some vital trail information to ensure we're well-prepared for our adventure on the Pillbox Hike.

Firstly, let's talk difficulty level. The Pillbox Hike falls into the moderate category, offering a balanced mix of challenge and enjoyment. While there are some steep sections along the way, they're manageable with a bit of determination and careful footing.

Next, let's discuss distance. The round-trip distance spans approximately 1.8 miles (2.9 km), making it an ideal outing for those seeking a moderate hike. Depending on your pace and how far you decide to venture, the hike typically takes around 1 to 1.5 hours to complete. If you're aiming to reach the first old military pillbox bunker, you can expect to arrive in about 20 to 30 minutes, setting the tone for the remainder of your journey (Lanikai Pillbox Hike - Breathtaking Views - Know before You Go, n.d.).

Now, let's address the elevation gain. As you ascend towards the pillboxes, you'll encounter a noticeable elevation gain of about 500 feet. This gradual climb adds an exciting dimension to the hike, offering stunning panoramic views as your reward for conquering the incline.

Lastly, let's not forget about sun exposure. Given the open terrain of the trail, it's essential to be mindful of sun exposure. Remember to pack sunscreen and wear a hat to shield yourself from the sun's rays as you traverse the picturesque landscape.

Permits and Regulations

Now, let's talk about permits and regulations, crucial aspects to consider before embarking on the Pillbox Hike.

Firstly, let's address permits. Technically, this hike falls under government property, and venturing without a permit is considered trespassing. While many folks might opt to skip this step, obtaining a permit is a straightforward process and costs a mere $2.50 (Frazer, 2024). It's a small investment for a smoother, legally sound adventure, so I highly recommend grabbing one to be on the safe side.

Moving on to regulations, respecting posted guidelines is key to maintaining the integrity of the trail. Although the trail is on state land, it's noteworthy that it's not part of the managed inventory of DLNR's Na Ala Hele and Access Program. This distinction underlines the importance of adhering to any specific rules outlined for this particular area (Lanikai Pillbox Trail, n.d.).

When it comes to technology, flying drones on the Lanikai Pillbox hike is a no-go. Laws surrounding drones in private areas make this activity illegal and should be avoided to ensure a harmonious hiking experience.

Additionally, a friendly reminder: it's advised against hiking to the Lanikai pillboxes from the back way. This route crosses private property and isn't regularly maintained, emphasizing the importance of sticking to the established trail for both safety and courtesy.

Parking and Entry Fee

Now, let's look into the practicalities of parking and entry for the Lanikai Pillbox hike, crucial details for a hassle-free adventure.

Firstly, the good news—there's no entry fee for this hike, making it an accessible option for all. Additionally, parking is free, but here's where the strategic planning comes in. Parking spaces can be limited, so it's essential to plan ahead and park legally on residential streets.

As you approach the trailheads located in neighborhoods, remember that there are no designated parking lots. Instead, you'll be navigating the residential streets for a suitable spot. In this scenario, it's paramount to be considerate to the local residents. Ensure you're following parking laws diligently—park a few feet from driveways, adhere to parking signs, and avoid blocking driveways or mailboxes.

For those embarking on a sunrise hike, a little extra courtesy goes a long way. Lock your car from the inside, especially if your car's locking mechanism produces a loud noise. This simple step ensures you don't inadvertently disturb residents who might still be catching some shut-eye.

It's crucial not to underestimate the importance of abiding by the rules—avoid parking in bike lanes, which could result in a hefty $200 fine. Remember, the later you arrive in the day, the more challenging parking might become. So, arm yourself with patience and be prepared to circle around a bit to find that perfect spot. A small effort in parking conscientiously ensures everyone enjoys the serenity of the trail without any unnecessary disruptions.

Navigation

Now, let's talk about navigating the Lanikai Pillbox hike. Knowing where you're going ensures a smoother, more enjoyable trek.

Firstly, the trailhead location is a key piece of the puzzle. Familiarize yourself with it, as the hike starts from Ka'elepulu Drive. If you're on the North Shore of Oahu Island for the Ehukai Pillbox Hike, the trailhead sits conveniently in the parking lot of Sunset Beach Elementary School. Look for a small sign pointing towards the forest—that's your starting point. Once on the trail, it's fairly straightforward, but here's a nugget of wisdom: when you reach the first pillbox, always stay left (Groves, 2021).

Now, for a bit of trail insight—the second pillbox is along the ridge, not higher up the mountain. So, continue along the edge of the ridge, heading north to reach the second pillbox. The trail might be well-worn, but clarity is king.

Talking about clarity, the trail is generally well-marked, yet having a map or using a navigation app can be a reassuring companion. While the trail markers are there, a little extra help can never hurt, especially if you're new to the terrain.

In essence, knowing your way around adds a layer of confidence to your journey. Keep these pointers in mind, and you'll be navigating the Lanikai Pillbox hike like a pro.

Gear and Equipment

Now, let's get practical about the gear and equipment you'll need for the Lanikai Pillbox hike. Keeping it simple, yet packing the essentials is the key to completing the hike successfully.

Firstly, proper clothing is your baseline—light layers, moisture-wicking, and attire suitable for the trail. Moving on to the feet, sturdy hiking shoes are your trusty sidekicks, especially for the steep and rocky terrain. Opt for tough yet light hiking boots for that ideal mix of ankle support, waterproofing, and durability.

A hat, whether it's a sun hat or a baseball cap, becomes your shield against the island sun. Don't forget those sunglasses, and consider rocking long sleeves for added sun protection.

Hydration is non-negotiable, so ensure you've got ample water with you. A small first-aid kit can be a handy companion for any minor bumps along the way. Given Hawaii's unpredictable weather, a lightweight rain jacket is a smart addition to your kit—versatile, compact, and ready for sudden weather changes.

Hiking poles are optional, tailored to those who prefer the extra support. As for snacks, a little energy boost during the hike is advisable, but keep it light—this isn't a marathon.

I would definitely advise you to pack light. Bring along a super-light hiking day pack and leave behind anything you won't absolutely need. While it's a short hike, one thing you definitely can't skimp on is water. Hawaii's sun and heat are no joke, and staying hydrated is your golden rule. Drink plenty before, during, and after your hike—it's your best companion on this island adventure.

Safety Precautions

When it comes to safety on the Lanikai Pillbox hike, a little caution goes a long way. Firstly, mind the steep sections, especially during descent—they can be challenging, particularly for little ones. If you're bringing kids along, ensure you're prepared to carry them if needed, or consider using hand-holding, a harness, or even a rope for added safety.

As you start walking on the trail, pay extra attention to the initial stretch, which is slippery and steep. Watch your step, as some areas have unstable rocks, posing potential tripping hazards.

Now, let's talk furry companions. While dogs are a common sight on hikes, consider the conditions before bringing them along. Signs and online warnings caution about dogs overheating, with some unfortunate incidents reported on this trail (Smith, 2023). If you decide to bring your pup, heed the advice and pack plenty of water to keep them cool and hydrated—after all, hiking in a fur coat under the sun sounds brutal, doesn't it?

Moving on to the pillboxes themselves, exercise caution. These structures are over 80 years old and show signs of wear and tear, with rusty parts and uneven surfaces. Be mindful of your surroundings and watch out for potential hazards.

Lastly, let's address the bees. The trail is lined with dragon fruit cacti, attracting thousands of honeybees during their blooming season. While you can't avoid them entirely, you can keep them from bothering you by staying calm and focused on your hike (Smith, 2023). So, if you're hitting the trail during blooming season, take note and prepare accordingly.

Water and Food

I cannot stress this enough, but staying hydrated is crucial on the Lanikai Pillbox hike, especially in the tropical climate. Make sure to bring enough water to keep you refreshed throughout the journey. When it comes to snacks, opt for healthy choices like nuts, seeds, fruits, or energy bars—popular options include Larabars, favored by many hikers.

If you're going on an early morning hike, consider packing a light breakfast, perhaps a sandwich or a protein bar, to fuel your adventure. For a delightful post-hike experience, think about bringing a picnic lunch or a snack to enjoy at a nearby beach or restaurant. After all, replenishing your energy is just as important as conquering the trail itself.

Timing

For the best experience on the Pillbox Hike, timing is key. It's wise to kick off your adventure early in the morning to relish cooler temperatures and beat the crowds. The hike typically lasts about 1 to 1.5 hours roundtrip, depending on your pace and how far you venture. Most hikers can reach the first pillbox in roughly 20 to 30 minutes, with the second pillbox just a 10-minute walk along the ridge.

To fully enjoy the stunning sunrise views from the mountaintop, consider starting your hike early in the morning. If you aren't an early bird, catch the sunrise from Lanikai Beach before heading up to the trail afterward. Plus, sticking to the cooler parts of the day helps you avoid the scorching sun, ensuring a more pleasant hiking experience.

Keep in mind to conclude your hike before sunset for a safe descent back down the trail. By planning your timing thoughtfully, you can make the most of your Lanikai Pillbox adventure while staying comfortable and safe.

Physical Preparation

Before setting off on the Lanikai Pillbox Hike, it's essential to prepare yourself physically. Take a moment to assess your fitness level to ensure that the trail aligns with your abilities. While the hike is moderate, it's always wise to know your limits and be prepared. Never push yourself too far.

To help prevent injuries and ensure a more enjoyable hike, consider doing some light stretching as part of your warm-up routine before hitting the trail. Pre-hike stretches can include simple movements like calf stretches, hamstring stretches, and arm circles to loosen up your muscles and prepare them for the activity ahead.

After completing the hike, take some time to stretch again as part of your cool-down routine. These post-hike stretches can help prevent muscle soreness and aid in recovery.

Focus on stretching your calves, quads, hamstrings, and shoulders to alleviate any tension built up during the hike and promote flexibility.

By incorporating both pre-hike and after-hike stretches into your routine, you can help minimize the risk of injury and discomfort.

How to Reach to Pillbox Hike From Waikiki

Reaching the Pillbox Hike from Waikiki Beach offers a couple of transportation options, each with its own advantages. If you're driving, the journey takes approximately 40 minutes from Waikiki Beach to Lanikai. Once you arrive in Lanikai, the starting point for the hike is located on a small street off of Ka'elepupu Drive, conveniently situated across from the Mid-Pacific Country Club.

For those opting for public transit, taking a bus from Waikiki Beach to Lanikai is also feasible, albeit requiring a bit more time. The journey typically takes around 1 hour or more, depending on traffic and bus schedules. The starting point of the hike remains the same, on a small street off of Ka'elepupu Drive in Lanikai, across from the Mid-Pacific Country Club.

Several bus routes provide access to the Lanikai neighborhood. Bus 671 offers a direct route to Lanikai, making it a convenient option for reaching the hike. Alternatively, taking Bus 8 or 20 to Ala Moana Center and then transferring to Bus 67 provides another route, taking you over the Pali to the downtown area near Lanikai.

Another option is to take Bus 56 or 57, both starting at Ala Moana Shopping Center. The 56 bus heads to Kailua town, which is close to Lanikai, providing another convenient transportation option for reaching the Pillbox Hike.

Photo Opportunities During Pillbox Hike

During the Pillbox Hike, there are plenty of opportunities to capture memorable photos of the stunning surroundings. As you start off on the trail, you'll be greeted with sweeping views that include Lanikai Beach, Kailua, and the majestic Koʻolau Mountain Range. These panoramic vistas offer the perfect backdrop for your hiking adventure.

If you opt to hike during sunset, you're in for a treat. The golden hour casts a magical glow over the landscape, enhancing the beauty of the scenery and providing ideal lighting for photography enthusiasts.

As you progress along the trail, you'll encounter two pillboxes, each offering unique perspectives of the landscape. While the first pillbox provides a great view, the second one offers an even better vantage point, showcasing the stunning Bellows and Waimanalo Beaches from above.

The trail is picturesque because of the lush vegetation and fascinating rock formations that surround you the entire time you're hiking. These natural elements create a visually appealing setting, perfect for capturing memorable moments.

Keep your eyes open for local wildlife, such as wild boars, which occasionally roam the area. Spotting these creatures adds an exciting element to your hike and presents an opportunity for wildlife photography enthusiasts to capture unique shots of the fauna in their natural habitat.

Segue: As we wrap up our exploration of the Pillbox Hike and uncover the historical significance of the Lanikai Pillboxes, the adventure is far from over. In this chapter, we've talked about the scenic trails, the breathtaking views, and the captivating stories etched into the remnants of World War II. The Pillbox Hike provided a unique blend of history and nature, leaving us with memories and insights.

But hold on tight, for the journey continues underwater in the next chapter! Dive into the vibrant world beneath the ocean's surface as we delve into the art of snorkeling. Get ready to explore the vibrant coral reefs, encounter colorful marine life, and witness the wonders that await beneath the waves. So, grab your fins and snorkel; an aquatic adventure awaits you in the upcoming pages!

Chapter Five

Hanauma Bay

Hawaii is the island of big dreams for both islanders and guests.
—Sharon Linnea

Plan a journey beneath the surface, where the turquoise waters of Hanauma Bay reveal a world teeming with life and wonder. Here's a little something to give you inspiration—you, surrounded by the gentle lull of the Pacific, the soft caress of the island breeze, and the promise of an underwater paradise awaiting your discovery. We will be viewing Hanauma Bay, a protected marine life conservation area since 1967, not just as a chapter – but also as an invitation to immerse yourself in the vibrant realm below the surface.

In 1990, a significant transformation began, a commitment to restore the bay's once-neglected reefs. The City & County of Honolulu took the reins, blending public access, reef restoration, and education into the fabric of Hanauma Bay. The result? A harmonious sanctuary where nature and education coexist.

As we dive into this chapter, we'll look into the fascinating tale of Hanauma Bay, shaped by the remnants of an ancient volcanic cone, a testament to the island's geological story. Beyond the scenic allure, this bay served as a retreat for Hawaiian royalty, echoing with the whispers of a bygone era.

But let's not linger on the shores for too long – the real magic lies beneath the waves. From essential tips for beginners to navigating the bay's unique conditions, I'm here to equip you for an unforgettable snorkeling escapade. Discover the marine wonders that grace the bay, and learn how to engage with them responsibly, ensuring both your safety and the preservation of this aquatic haven.

So, whether you're a seasoned snorkeler or dipping your fins for the first time, join us as we navigate the crystal-clear waters of Hanauma Bay, unlocking the secrets of its vibrant marine life and exploring the delicate balance between nature, education, and adventure. The journey awaits, and the bay beckons with open arms. Let's dive in together!

Snorkeling Tips

As we gear up for our underwater adventure at Hanauma Bay, it's essential to equip ourselves with the right snorkeling gear and techniques. Whether you're a seasoned snorkeler or dipping your toes into the aquatic realm for the first time, these tips are your compass for a safe and enjoyable experience.

Let's start with the basics of your underwater arsenal – the mask, fins, and snorkel. Finding the perfect fit for your mask is crucial. Ensure the mask snugly covers your eyes and the strap rests comfortably around the widest part of your head. A quick 'mask test' will confirm if it's a secure fit without being too tight.

To combat the notorious fogging issue, defog your mask using baby shampoo or defogging gel. Visibility is key, and a fog-free mask ensures an uninterrupted underwater spectacle. Learning to clear excess water from your mask is a vital skill. Practice doing so before venturing into the water, and remember, there's no need to panic if your mask fills up. Surface calmly, clear the water, and resume your exploration.

For Beginners

For those taking their first plunge into snorkeling, a few additional tips can make a world of difference. Full-foot fins are recommended for beginners, providing underwater mobility without the hassle of adjustable straps. Preserving energy and ensuring the right fit are the keys to fin success.

Breathing becomes an art underwater, and taking deep, focused breaths is your ticket to relaxation. The snorkeling experience may limit your breathing, so mastering this technique is crucial for a calm and enjoyable journey beneath the waves.

For Non-Swimmers

Even if you haven't mastered the art of swimming, snorkeling at Hanauma Bay is still within reach. Choose calm waters, invest in a snorkeling vest for added buoyancy, and breathe slowly to maintain composure. The right equipment, careful destination selection, and never snorkeling alone are vital considerations for non-swimmers.

So, whether you're adjusting your mask for a perfect fit or practicing the 'moon walk' into the ocean with fins secured, these snorkeling tips ensure that your underwater excursion at Hanauma Bay is a blend of safety, relaxation, and pure aquatic delight. Ready to explore? Let's dive in together!

About Hanauma Bay

Before you begin your underwater adventure, let's dive into essential information to ensure a memorable and safe experience.

Snorkeling Information

Before you dip into the crystal-clear waters, check the current snorkeling conditions for optimal visibility and water clarity. Keep an eye out for the vibrant marine life that calls Hanauma Bay home, including tropical fish and colorful coral reefs.

Permits and Regulations

Navigating Hanauma Bay comes with a set of guidelines to ensure a seamless and enjoyable experience. The Nature Preserve operates from Wednesdays through Sundays, welcoming visitors from 6:45 a.m. to 1:30 p.m. It's crucial to adhere to this timeframe, with a mandatory exit by 4 p.m. and beach clearance by 3:30 p.m. Be aware that these hours may change, necessitating a call to (808) 768-6861 for the latest updates.

To streamline your visit, consider utilizing the Parks & Recreation Online System (PROS), which allows you to reserve entry times and make online payments. As of now reservations are required to enter. The key is that you can only reserve your spot three days in advance. If you are on the island, make a reminder to get in first thing in the morning 3 days before you plan to visit. Keep in mind that reservations are non-transferable and non-refundable, emphasizing the need for careful planning. For Hawai'i residents with valid identification, the reserve-entry requirement does not apply, except for non-Hawai'i residents accompanied by kama'āina or military members without Hawai'i identification.

Reservations and payments are accepted for groups of up to 10 people, with a mix of children and adults. A 2.35% service fee is applied to online payments, while parking fees can be settled on-site using cash. A confirmation email is sent upon reservation, requiring a matching photo ID for entry, emphasizing the non-transferable nature of reservations.

As of July 1, 2023, Hawai'i residents can access the preserve without a reservation during public hours. However, this exemption doesn't apply to non-residents, even if accompanied by kama'āina or military members. For those without online access, limited walk-in or drive-in entry is permitted, with on-site payment options available. An educational video must be watched for each visit, ensuring visitors are well-informed about conservation efforts and safety measures. Always remember that unauthorized use of reservations voids them without a refund, underscoring the importance of compliance with these regulations for the collective enjoyment and preservation of Hanauma Bay.

Snorkeling Gear

If you don't have your own gear, don't fret! On-site snorkeling equipment rentals are available. Ensure you wear appropriate swimwear for snorkeling to enhance your underwater experience.

Safety Precautions

Safety first! Familiarize yourself with the locations of lifeguard stations and adhere to their instructions. Protect the delicate coral ecosystem by refraining from touching or standing on coral formations. Avoid hazardous areas and supervise children at all times.

Facilities

Hanauma Bay offers various amenities for a comfortable visit, including restroom facilities, showers, picnic areas, a snack bar, gift shop, and locker rentals. Lifeguards are stationed throughout the preserve, ensuring your safety. The facilities are wheelchair accessible, ensuring everyone can enjoy the beauty of Hanauma Bay.

How to Reach Hanauma Bay from Waikiki Beach

Finding your way from the bustling shores of Waikiki Beach to the tranquil haven of Hanauma Bay offers several transportation options. For those inclined toward public transit, consider hopping on either the Waikiki Trolley Blue Line or Route 22, commonly known as the Beach Bus. The Waikiki Trolley Blue Line treats passengers to a scenic journey along Oahu's southeastern coastline, with an approximate travel time of 1 hour and 15 minutes. Simultaneously, Route 22 shuttles between Waikiki and Hanauma Bay within a similar time frame. The cost for these buses is $2.75 for adults and $1.25 for children, offering an affordable and picturesque travel experience.

Alternatively, if time is of the essence, taxis stand out as the quickest and most convenient means of reaching Hanauma Bay. However, it's essential to keep in mind that taxi fares may be relatively higher compared to bus travel. For those who prefer the freedom of driving, the journey takes approximately 30-40 minutes, presenting an opportunity to explore Oahu at your own pace. Parking at Hanauma Bay incurs a $3 fee per vehicle, ensuring a secure spot for your convenience.

No matter the mode of transportation you choose, each offers its unique experience en route to the aquatic wonders of Hanauma Bay. As you transition from the vibrant energy of Waikiki Beach to the serene beauty of the bay, anticipate the breathtaking journey that awaits you at one of Oahu's most cherished snorkeling destinations.

Cost of Snorkeling

Snorkeling in Hanauma Bay includes an entry fee of $25 per person for individuals aged 13 and above. Additional costs may apply for optional snorkeling accessories, or you can bring your own gear. Keep in mind that the park is closed on Mondays and Tuesdays, so plan your visit accordingly.

Things to Do

Hanauma Bay offers a myriad of activities for visitors seeking a day of exploration and relaxation. With over 400 species of marine life, snorkeling takes center stage as one of the bay's most popular and immersive experiences. Whether renting gear on-site or bringing personal equipment, visitors can dive into the clear, protected waters and encounter vibrant aquatic life, from tangs and trumpet fish to the iconic Hawaiian green sea turtle.

Beyond snorkeling, the bay beckons with opportunities for a refreshing swim in its crystal-clear sanctuary. Before embarking on aquatic adventures, visitors are required to engage in a brief yet essential ritual – a mandatory 9-minute safety video. This educational snippet imparts knowledge on proper snorkeling techniques and emphasizes the significance of preserving the delicate coral ecosystem.

For those seeking a more laid-back day, the bay's pristine white sand beach provides an idyllic setting. Visitors can bask in the sun, though shade is limited, prompting the wise inclusion of sun protection like hats, sunglasses, and umbrellas in their beach essentials.

For the land enthusiasts, Hanauma Bay extends its allure beyond the shoreline. Nearby trails, such as the Koko Head Crater and Makapu'u Lighthouse, offer hiking opportunities amidst breathtaking landscapes. Whether it's the allure of underwater exploration or the tranquility of sun-soaked shores, Hanauma Bay ensures a diverse array of activities for every visitor's preference.

Marine Life Encounters

Diving into the underwater realm of Hanauma Bay reveals a vibrant tapestry of marine life, each species contributing to the bay's ecological richness. One of the most cherished inhabitants is the green sea turtle, often spotted gracefully navigating the waters or resting near the coral reefs. Respecting their protected status under both Hawaiian and federal law is crucial; observing these gentle creatures from a safe distance ensures their well-being.

The bay's diverse fish community presents a colorful spectacle. Parrotfish, surgeonfish, triggerfish, butterfly fish, damselfish, angelfish, and wrasses are among the enchanting species that captivate snorkelers. Their vibrant hues and intricate patterns create a mesmerizing underwater display.

Hanauma Bay isn't solely about fish and sea turtles; it's a bustling community of invertebrates like sea urchins, sea cucumbers, and crabs. These often-overlooked creatures play a vital role in maintaining the health of the coral reefs, contributing to the bay's overall ecological balance.

Beyond the expected residents, Hanauma Bay surprises visitors with occasional appearances by dolphins and humpback whales, particularly during their respective seasons. These majestic marine giants add an extra layer of wonder to the snorkeling experience.

To make the most of these encounters, timing is key. While the park welcomes visitors from 6 am to 7 pm, mornings offer the best snorkeling conditions. Calmer waters and enhanced visibility make for an optimal underwater exploration. Considering the conservation efforts limiting daily visitors, early arrival becomes strategic, especially during peak seasons. By embracing the wonders of Hanauma Bay with mindfulness and awe, visitors contribute to the preservation of this marine haven.

Pictures and Photo Op at Hanauma Bay

For those eager to capture the beauty of Hanauma Bay, guided snorkel tours offered by various companies present an enticing opportunity for underwater photography. These tours not only facilitate a more structured and informed snorkeling experience but also enhance the chances of capturing stunning underwater moments.

It's important to note, however, that Hanauma Bay might not be the ideal choice if your photographic focus leans toward corals and underwater topography. The bay features limited live coral, and occasional low visibility—especially on windy days—can pose challenges for capturing intricate details. As you decide to go on these guided tours, the emphasis may shift towards the vibrant marine life and the overall enchanting atmosphere, offering a different but equally rewarding perspective for your photographic endeavors.

Segue: In this chapter, we've delved deep into the world of snorkeling at Hanauma Bay, exploring essential tips, safety measures, and the vibrant marine life that awaits. Remember the importance of respecting the marine environment and maximizing your snorkeling experience during peak times. Now, get ready to ride the waves as we dive into the exhilarating world of surfing in the next chapter. Discover the techniques, gear, and adrenaline-pumping adventures that await you on the waves of Hawaii's iconic surf spots.

Share the Aloha Spirit with Your Review: Your Words Can Spark a Journey of Discovery

Hawaii isn't just a place; it's a vibrant tapestry of culture, adventure, and natural beauty. Remember, the true essence of Aloha is sharing and caring without expecting anything in return.

Imagine if you could light up someone's journey to Oahu with just a few words. That's the magic we're inviting you to create today.

So, I've got a little favor to ask...

Would you be willing to share a slice of your Oahu adventure by writing a review? Think of it as sending a postcard to a friend who's about to embark on a journey you've just returned from.

By sharing your experience with The Oahu Travel and Adventure Guide, you're not just leaving a review. You're becoming a part of someone else's adventure, guiding them towards those hidden gems and unforgettable moments that you discovered.

Our goal is to make every trip to Oahu an extraordinary one. But to do that, we need to reach out and touch the hearts of travelers everywhere.

And here's where you come in. Your review could be the beacon that guides one more traveler to:

★ Dive into the heart of Oahu's culture beyond the usual tourist trails.

★ Support local shops and eateries that are the soul of the island.

★ Discover the serene beauty of hidden beaches and secret spots.

★ Make connections with the locals that turn into lifelong friendships.

★ Experience the adventure of a lifetime that they'll treasure forever.

Taking the time to share your thoughts is a gift that costs nothing but can change someone's experience in ways you can't even imagine. Plus, you'll get that warm, fuzzy feeling knowing you've helped light the way for another explorer.

Here's how you can spread the Aloha Spirit in just 60 seconds: Leave your review by scanning the QR code below:

I can't wait to see the amazing stories and adventures your review will inspire. Together, let's make every journey to Oahu a voyage of discovery and connection.

Mahalo nui loa (thank you very much) for your kindness and support. Now, let's dive back into the adventures that await!

Chapter Six

Surfing and the North Shore

For me, the magic of Hawaii comes from the stillness, the sea, the stars. —Joanne Harris

Welcome to the vibrant world of surfing at North Shore, Oahu, where the rhythmic dance of waves beckons adventurers from around the globe. Situated on the easternmost side of the island, North Shore Oahu is a paradise of picturesque beaches, lush tropical forests, and legendary surf breaks. Stretching over 17 miles from Ka'ena Point to Kahuku Point, this coastal wonderland boasts iconic spots like Waimea Bay, 'Ehukai Beach (Banzai Pipeline), and Sunset Beach (Dimple, 2023a).

As you embark on this exhilarating chapter, prepare to ride the waves and immerse yourself in the essence of Hawaiian surf culture. Whether you're a seasoned surfer seeking adrenaline-pumping rides or a beginner eager to catch your first wave, North Shore offers an array of experiences to suit every skill level.

Join us as we explore the best surf spots, uncover the secrets of each location's unique characteristics, and dive into the exhilarating world of North Shore surfing. From the legendary barrels of Pipeline to the rolling swells of Sunset Beach, each wave holds a story waiting to be told.

So, grab your board, feel the ocean breeze on your face, and get ready to experience the magic of surfing at North Shore, where the sea whispers tales of adventure and the waves beckon you to dance with them.

Best Surf Spots

When it comes to surfing, the North Shore of Oahu is renowned worldwide for its legendary surf spots, each offering a unique experience for wave riders of all levels. Let's dive into some of the best surf spots that define the thrilling surf culture of North Shore:

Banzai Pipeline (Ehukai Beach Park): Known as the "Banzai Pipeline," this iconic surf spot boasts barreling waves that attract the best and bravest surfers. While winter brings massive swells, creating challenging conditions, summer offers calmer waters suitable for a refreshing dip ("Ehukai Beach Park (Banzai Pipeline)," 2018). Just be sure to check in with the lifeguards for the latest conditions before hitting the waves.

Sunset Beach: With its long stretches of rideable surf, Sunset Beach is a favorite among families and big-wave enthusiasts alike. During winter, spectators can witness awe-inspiring waves reaching up to 30 feet, alongside premier surfing competitions (Sunset Beach, n.d.). In the summer, the beach transforms into a serene haven perfect for swimming and snorkeling.

Waimea Bay: Renowned for its towering 30-foot waves in winter, Waimea Bay is a mecca for experienced surfers seeking adrenaline-pumping rides. During the summer months, the bay offers tranquil waters ideal for various water activities, including swimming, snorkeling, and diving (Waimea Bay, 2017).

Rocky Point: As one of the most high-performance waves on the North Shore, Rocky Point attracts Hawaii's best locals and top surfers worldwide. On any given day with swell, you'll witness incredible surfing prowess as surfers conquer this dynamic surf spot.

Laniakea (Turtle Beach): Beyond its breathtaking panoramic views, Laniakea Beach, also known as Turtle Beach, is home to the beloved sea turtles. While surfers chase waves, visitors are captivated by the charm of these gentle creatures basking on the shore.

Chun's Reef: With its long sandy beach and gentle waves, Chun's Reef offers a welcoming environment for surfers of all levels. Families can enjoy the serene freshwater pond while surf schools and experienced riders take on the waves.

Gas Chambers: Offering consistent surf conditions, Gas Chambers is a popular spot for surfers seeking thrilling rides. Although it can get crowded, the epic waves make it worth the wait.

Log Cabins: Nestled on the North Shore, Log Cabins offers a challenging yet rewarding surfing experience, with gnarly waves breaking over a lava reef bottom.

Off The Wall: Known for its epic barreling waves, Off the Wall draws surfers and fans alike with its captivating surf culture and dynamic waves.

Haleiwa Beach: Located at the western end of the Seven-Mile Miracle, Haleiwa Beach is revered for its hollow rights and powerful closeouts, making it a favorite among experienced surfers.

While some spots, like Pipeline and Backdoor, are strictly for professionals, Turtle Bay provides a safe haven for beginners. Whether you're seeking adrenaline-fueled rides or serene waters, North Shore's diverse surf spots offer something for everyone, ensuring an unforgettable surfing experience amidst Oahu's stunning coastline.

Surfing Lessons for All Levels

Going on a surfing adventure on the North Shore of Oahu is not just a thrill; it's an art, and these reputable surf schools stand ready to turn every novice into a wave-riding expert. Let's dive into the sea of possibilities with some outstanding options.

North Shore Oahu Surf School

Situated in the laid-back town of Haleiwa, the North Shore Oahu Surf School is a haven for surf enthusiasts of all ages and levels. Offering individual, group, and private lessons, their commitment shines through with a 100% satisfaction guarantee – a testament to their confidence in turning every student into a wave conqueror. As the rhythmic waves of the Pacific provide the soundtrack, this school promises an experience that echoes the true spirit of North Shore surfing.

North Shore Ohana School of Surfing

For those seeking a more intimate surfing experience, the North Shore Ohana School of Surfing beckons with private lessons, 2-surfer private lessons, and group lessons tailored to all skill levels. With flexibility in timing, free cancellation options, and a good money-back guarantee if you don't find yourself upright on a surfboard, this school epitomizes the 'Ohana' spirit, welcoming everyone into the surfing family.

Hans Hedemann Surf School

Located in the vibrant Waikiki, the Hans Hedemann Surf School extends its expertise to the North Shore, offering hourly lessons, surf camps, and private lessons. Their commitment to both beginners and advanced surfers sets the stage for skill enhancement against the backdrop of Waikiki's iconic waves. With a focus on improvement, Hans Hedemann Surf School invites surf enthusiasts to ride the waves and elevate their surfing prowess.

North Shore Surf Girls

Breaking the traditional mold, North Shore Surf Girls takes the waves by storm, offering beginner surfing lessons and stand-up paddleboarding lessons for individuals and families alike. Their inclusivity is reflected in the range of options – group, semi-private, and private lessons – accommodating diverse schedules. As the sun kisses the waves, North Shore Surf Girls invites everyone to embrace the surfing journey, fostering a community of wave riders.

Uncle Bryan's Sunset Suratt Surf

Rooted in family traditions, Uncle Bryan's Sunset Suratt Surf brings a touch of familial warmth to the surfing scene. As a family-owned surf school, they offer lessons and paddleboard adventures for all ages and skill levels. With a commitment to creating a fun and safe learning environment, Uncle Bryan's invites beginners and seasoned surfers alike to catch the waves and master the art of surfing in the heart of the North Shore.

These surf schools embody the essence of North Shore's surfing culture, blending skill development with a sense of community and fun. Whether you're stepping onto a surfboard for the first time or seeking to refine your technique, these schools ensure that your North Shore surfing experience is nothing short of extraordinary.

Surf Lessons in Waikiki

Before you dive into the rhythm of the Pacific waves at Waikiki, let's ensure your journey is as smooth as the gentle lapping of the ocean. Honolulu's Waikiki Beach beckons with its white sandy shores and legendary landmarks, promising an adventure that will linger in your memories.

Arrival Instructions and the Island Beat

As you start your Waikiki escapade, most visitors find their way through the embrace of Honolulu International Airport, a mere nine miles south of Waikiki. From here, the island unfurls its charms, and your choice of travel plays a significant role. Whether you opt for the freedom of car rentals, the ease of taxis, the laid-back charm of public transit, or the convenience of private shuttles, your journey to the beach begins with these options.

For those steering their own course, Interstate H-1 awaits, offering a route through McCully Street or the busier Nimitz Highway 92. While H-1 might be the busiest in Hawaii, it's your gateway to the vibrant pulse of Waikiki.

Navigating the Island

Once you've touched down in paradise, the question becomes – how to weave through the vibrant tapestry of Waikiki? While traffic may ripple along Ala Moana Boulevard and Kalakaua Avenue, fear not, for driving in Waikiki is generally a breeze. But, it's worth noting that Honolulu boasts one of the most notorious traffic congestions in the

U.S. Fear not, though, alternatives dance at your fingertips. The Waikiki Trolley, The Bus, and a fleet of other trolleys and tour buses stand ready to usher you through the streets, ensuring you don't miss a beat.

Cost of Surfing Lessons

As you stand on the golden sands, gazing at the azure horizon, the call of the waves becomes irresistible. The cost of surf lessons and equipment rental at Waikiki Beach, however, varies like the shades of the Pacific.

Waikīkī Beach Services: This beachfront haven offers daily surf and stand-up paddleboard lessons, with prices as soothing as the ocean breeze. Explore their offerings on for a glimpse into your aquatic adventure.

Surf In The City: With lessons starting at 9:00 AM daily, Surf In The City invites you to ride the waves at your pace. Surfboard and stand-up paddleboard rentals await, with prices tailored to your needs. Connect with them directly at for the key to your surfing kingdom.

Big Wave Dave Surf Co.: For those seeking the freedom to ride the waves by the hour, Big Wave Dave Surf Co. extends a welcome. Whether a day, week, or the entirety of your vacation, their surfboard rentals promise flexibility. Unveil the details at for a surfing experience on your terms.

Beach Boy Hale: At Beach Boy Hale, various beach rentals, including surfboard rentals, await your selection. Opt for delivery to your hotel, ensuring a seamless transition from sand to surf. Connect with them directly at for a beachside rendezvous.

Star Beachboys: With surfboard rentals at $10 per hour, Star Beachboys invites you to immerse yourself in the rhythm of Waikiki. Additional hours beckon for those unwilling to part with the ocean's embrace. Dive into specifics at their surf shop or reach out directly for an oceanic rendezvous.

As you traverse the golden shores and feel the pulse of the ocean, let these details guide your journey into the heart of Waikiki's surfing symphony. The waves await, and your adventure is poised to become a harmonious blend of skill, sea, and serenity.

Surfing Tips for Beginners and Safety Guidelines

Surfing, the dance between sea and surfer, begins with respect for the ocean's rhythm. For beginners seeking the embrace of the waves, here are some tips to navigate the learning curve:

- Seeking wisdom from a surf school or instructor forms the foundation of your journey. These mentors unravel the secrets of the waves, teaching not just the basics but also instilling crucial safety guidelines.

- The artistry of surfing extends beyond the waves. Begin by practicing pop-ups out of the water, refining your technique on solid ground. This terrestrial rehearsal primes you for the fluid dance awaiting in the ocean.

- Before diving in, observe the ocean's poetry. Watch how waves break, acquaint yourself with sandbars, and decipher the language of the sea. Reading the ocean becomes your compass, guiding you to the perfect wave.

- Surfing is a communal experience, and understanding the unspoken rules is crucial. Pay attention to fellow surfers, noting their positions in the water. Respect their space, and the ocean's harmony becomes a collective masterpiece.

- Starting on a bigger board, like a longboard, serves as your stepping stone. Larger boards make wave-catching more accessible and provide stability as you rise to stand. It's the steady platform you need as you acquaint yourself with the dance of balance.

- Seek solitude for your practice, away from crowded waters. Understand your limits and respect the spaces of others. Your learning journey is personal, but it's vital to remain considerate of those sharing the waves.

- Waves, like life, are rarely perfect. Embrace the opportunity to ride even the imperfect ones. Each wave, regardless of its form, contributes to your evolution as a surfer.

As you delve into the art of surfing, safety becomes your steadfast companion. Here's a code of conduct to ensure every ride is not just thrilling but secure:

- **Always wear a leash.** This simple accessory keeps your board close, averting potential hazards and ensuring a shared harmony among surfers.

- **The ocean, vast and alluring, demands respect.** Leave ample space for fellow surfers, acknowledging the shared arena where waves unite all. Disturb not the rhythm of others.

- **In the dance of waves, priority rules dictate order.** Understand the hierarchy, ensuring you don't paddle through the heart of the break. Respectful navigation is the key.

- **The solitude of the sea is best shared.** Avoid the solitude of solo surfing; always inform someone about your surfing destination. The ocean is vast, and unity ensures safety.

- **As you surf, be mindful of your surroundings.** Comprehend the currents and identify unsurfable waves. Awareness transcends the dance; it ensures you navigate the sea's nuances.

- **Surfing is about fluidity, not obstacles.** Steer clear of areas with rocks or shallow waters. Your safety and the preservation of your board depend on smooth waters.

- **If caught in a rip current, panic is the adversary.** Swim parallel to the shore until free of the current's grasp. Rationality guides you through nature's challenges.

Start your surfing journey not just as a rider of waves but as a custodian of the ocean's grace. Let each lesson, each wave, etch a tale of respect, wisdom, and shared joy on the canvas of your surfing odyssey.

Segue: As we bid adieu to the thrilling surf breaks of North Shore, our chapter on surfing unfolds as a tale of mastering the relationship between surfer and sea. From the iconic Pipeline's barreling waves to the serene shores of Haleiwa, we've explored the spectrum of this aquatic playground. For beginners, we paved a pathway with tips and safety guidelines, and for the adept, we uncovered the secrets of North Shore's renowned surf spots.

In the rhythm of the waves, we learned that surfing is more than a sport; it's an immersive journey into the heart of the ocean. Safety and respect for the sea became our guiding stars, leading us through the exhilarating highs and humbling lows of the surfing adventure. Each wave, a chapter in its own right, taught us resilience, patience, and the sheer joy of conquering the mighty Pacific.

But as one chapter concludes, another beckons on the horizon. In the upcoming pages, we shift our focus from the crests of waves to the gentle currents of the sea. Join me as we discuss the art of kayaking, exploring the coastal wonders of Oahu's shores. The ocean, ever a masterful storyteller, unveils new tales with every stroke of the paddle.

Chapter Seven

Kayaking to Mokulua Islands

Life should not be a journey to the grave with the intention of arriving safely in a pretty and well preserved body, but rather to skid in broadside in a cloud of smoke, thoroughly used up, totally worn out, and loudly proclaiming "Wow! What a Ride!" —Hunter S. Thompson

W elcome to a chapter that echoes the spirit of Thompson's words. As we begin the exhilarating voyage of kayaking, let us embrace the thrill of the ride, the rhythm of the waves, and the serenity of the sea. Our destination? The breathtaking Mokulua Islands, affectionately known as "The Mokes" by locals, beckon us from afar.

Nestled off Wailea Point on Oahu's windward side, these twin isles stand as timeless sentinels of nature's grandeur. Moku Nui, the larger of the two, rises majestically with a volcanic cone reaching 225 feet above the azure waters. Its counterpart, Moku Iki, a solitary hump peaking at 150 feet, stands in quiet reverence, a sanctuary untouched by human footprints (Oahu Activities Expert, n.d.).

But before we set sail to explore these hidden gems, let's equip ourselves with the essentials of kayaking. From life vests that ensure our safety to paddles that propel us forward, we'll talk about the gear required for a seamless voyage. Additionally, we'll uncover optional accessories and clothing, from paddle leashes to wetsuits, ensuring comfort and preparedness for every journey.

As we navigate the pristine waters en route to the Mokulua Islands, we'll not only indulge in the thrill of adventure but also embrace responsible kayaking practices. With each stroke of the paddle, we'll tread lightly upon the ocean, respecting its delicate ecosystem and preserving its natural beauty for generations to come.

So, the Mokulua Islands await, ready to enchant us with their secluded beaches, hidden coves, and timeless allure. Let's dive into the world of kayaking and immerse ourselves in the wonder that lies beyond the horizon.

Kayaking Gear Guide

When venturing into the expansive realm of kayaking, proper gear becomes your trusty companion on the rhythmic dance of ocean waves. Let's explore the essential equipment that ensures your safety and enhances your kayaking experience.

Essential Gear

1. **Personal Flotation Device (PFD):** Your aquatic guardian, a PFD, or life vest, is non-negotiable. It keeps you buoyant and secures your safety.

2. **Paddle:** An extension of your intent, a reliable paddle becomes your partner in navigating the waters. Consider carrying a spare for longer journeys.

3. **Safety whistle:** A modest yet crucial tool for emergencies, the whistle is your audible lifeline, alerting others to your presence.

4. **Bilge pump:** A diligent assistant, the bilge pump evacuates any unwelcome water that sneaks into your kayak.

5. **Spray skirt:** For chilly waters or turbulent conditions, a spray skirt shields you from the elements.

6. **Dry bags:** Safeguard your essentials from unpredictable splashes, ensuring a dry and secure journey.

7. **First aid kit:** A pocket of reassurance, the first aid kit attends to unforeseen circumstances, embodying preparedness.

8. **Navigation tools:** For adventurers charting unexplored territories, a compass or GPS becomes your directional guide.

9. **Repair kit:** A patchwork of resilience, including duct tape, a multi-tool, and spare parts, ensures you tackle any unexpected hiccups.

Optional Gear

1. **Paddle leash:** A loyal companion, preventing your paddle from drifting away, especially after a capsize.

2. **Float bags:** These unassuming inflatables add stability and avert potential disaster, keeping your kayak afloat.

3. **Emergency flares or strobes:** Illuminating your presence in remote locales or low-visibility scenarios, these tools enhance safety.

4. **Two-way radios:** Bridges the silence in the vast expanse, fostering communication in group escapades.

5. **Fishing gear:** For angling enthusiasts, rod holders and tackle storage transform your kayak into a mobile fishing haven.

Whether you're embarking on a solo sojourn or joining a group expedition, these gear essentials and optional companions become your silent allies, shaping a secure and enjoyable kayaking escapade.

Clothing

When preparing for a kayaking adventure, your choice of clothing can make all the difference in ensuring both comfort and safety throughout your journey.

Wetsuit/Dry top: Depending on the temperature of the air and water, it's crucial to dress appropriately. A wetsuit or dry top provides insulation and protection against the elements, keeping you warm and dry even in chilly waters. Whether you opt for a full wetsuit or a dry top paired with suitable bottoms, the key is to choose garments that offer thermal regulation without restricting your movements.

Hat and sunscreen: The sun can be relentless, especially when you're out on the water for an extended period. A wide-brimmed hat not only shields your face and eyes from harsh UV rays but also helps regulate your body temperature by providing shade. Additionally, don't forget to generously apply sunscreen to exposed skin areas, including your face, neck, arms, and legs. Opt for a water-resistant sunscreen with a high SPF to ensure long-lasting protection against sunburn and skin damage.

River shoes: Stepping into the water or traversing rocky terrain demands footwear that can handle the challenge. River shoes are designed with durable materials and grippy soles to provide traction and stability on wet surfaces. Whether you're launching your kayak from a sandy beach, wading through shallow waters, or exploring rocky shores, river shoes offer the necessary protection and support for your feet. Choose a pair that fits snugly and offers adequate toe protection to prevent injuries while walking on diverse terrain.

By dressing thoughtfully and equipping yourself with the right clothing and accessories, you not only enhance your comfort and safety but also set the stage for an enjoyable and memorable kayaking experience.

Secluded Beaches and Hidden Coves

As you paddle along the turquoise waters, you'll discover a treasure trove of secluded beaches and hidden coves, each more breathtaking than the last.

Cockroach Cove (Halona Beach Cove): Accessible via a scenic hiking trail, Cockroach Cove enchants visitors with its crystal-clear waters and stunning vistas. Nestled amidst rugged cliffs, this hidden gem is a paradise for kayakers seeking tranquility and natural beauty.

Lanikai Beach: With its powdery white sand and clear turquoise waters, Lanikai Beach is a picturesque haven framed by the iconic Mokulua Islands. As you glide along the coastline, keep an eye out for sea turtles, as Lanikai Beach serves as a nesting ground for these magnificent creatures.

Bellows Field Beach Park: Set against the backdrop of the majestic Mokulua Islands, Bellows Field Beach Park offers a unique blend of sandy shores and lush greenery.

Moku Nui Island: Part of the Mokulua Islands State Park, Moku Nui Island entices kayakers with its pristine beaches and abundant marine life. Dive into the crystal-clear waters for a snorkeling adventure, or explore the island's hiking trails for panoramic views of the surrounding landscape.

Kalama Beach Park: A favorite destination for locals and visitors alike, Kalama Beach Park boasts sandy shores, grassy areas, and a protected marine life conservation area.

Kailua Beach Park: Stretching along a picturesque coastline, Kailua Beach Park invites kayakers to explore its long sandy beach, ideal for swimming, sunbathing, and leisurely strolls.

Secret Beach (Ali'inui Beach): Tucked away from the hustle and bustle, Secret Beach, also known as Ali'inui Beach, offers a peaceful retreat for kayakers seeking solitude. Whether you're swimming, sunbathing, or simply walking along the shoreline, Secret Beach promises a serene escape from the ordinary.

Responsible kayaking involves not only enjoying the natural beauty of the waterways but also ensuring minimal impact on the environment. Here are some essential tips for responsible kayaking, emphasizing the importance of respecting marine life and adhering to Leave No Trace principles:

- **Minimize noise pollution:** Paddle quietly to avoid disturbing marine life. Refrain from loud conversations and unnecessary noise. Respect the tranquility of the surroundings, especially in areas known for nesting birds and marine mammals.

- **Maintain a safe distance:** Keep a safe distance from wildlife to avoid causing stress or disruption. Use binoculars or a camera with a zoom lens for a closer look instead of approaching animals.

- **Avoid feeding wildlife:** Do not feed marine animals, as it disrupts their natural behavior and diet. Feeding wildlife can alter their habits and their dependency on humans for food.

- **Mind your paddle:** Be mindful of your paddle to avoid accidentally striking marine life, especially in shallow areas. Navigate carefully in seagrass beds and coral reefs to prevent damage to these delicate ecosystems.

- **Dispose of waste properly:** Pack out all trash, including wrappers, bottles, and any other waste generated during your kayaking adventure. Use designated waste disposal facilities and recycle when possible.

- **Follow Leave No Trace principles:** Stick to established water access points and launch sites to prevent erosion and damage to the shoreline. Leave natural and cultural features undisturbed, avoiding the removal of plants, rocks, or artifacts.

By incorporating these responsible kayaking tips into your adventure, you contribute to the preservation of marine ecosystems and ensure that future generations can enjoy the same natural beauty.

Segue: In this chapter, we've explored the essentials of kayaking gear, from life vests to navigation tools, and discussed the importance of responsible kayaking practices. We've highlighted the pristine beauty of the Mokulua Islands as a kayaking destination and shared tips for enjoying secluded beaches and hidden coves while respecting marine life and nature. As we bid farewell to the tranquil waters of the Mokulua Islands, our next adventure awaits in the wonders of Kailua Bay. Join us in the upcoming chapter as we delve into the enchanting landscapes, exciting activities, and hidden gems of Kailua Bay, promising yet another unforgettable journey along the shores of Hawaii.

Chapter Eight

Kailua Bay

The danger of adventure is worth a thousand days of ease and comfort. —Paulo Coelho

Nestled across the pier from Kamakahonu Bay, Kailua Bay beckons with its promise of diverse offerings and thrilling beach activities. Here, readers will embark on a journey through the vibrant waters of Kailua Beach, where kayaking, stand-up paddleboarding, windsurfing, kitesurfing, and surfing await.

As we delve into the practicalities, we'll uncover the amenities, directions, and essential knowledge needed for a safe and enjoyable experience.

At the heart of our exploration lies kayaking, where detailed insights await on equipment, safety measures, self-guided tours, and permits. Empowering readers to plan a seamless adventure, we'll navigate through wildlife awareness, snorkeling gear essentials, optimal timing, physical preparation, hydration tips, and beach etiquette. Along the shores of Kailua Bay, we'll discover not just an adventure but also a sanctuary for capturing timeless moments and creating cherished memories. So, let's dive in and embrace the exhilarating spirit of Kailua Bay, where every wave carries the promise of a thrilling escapade.

About Kailua Beach

Kalama Beach, affectionately known as Kalamas, emerges to the right of Kailua Beach Park. Transitioning from the bustling main park, Kalamas invites with a quieter charm. The lack of nearby services and the surrounding beachfront cottages and homes add to its local appeal. The serene atmosphere makes Kalama a haven for relaxation, distinguishing itself from the more activity-centric Kailua Beach Park.

Moving towards the far end, Castles Beach unveils itself, featuring a less crowded setting and a small surf break offshore. This section draws a laid-back crowd, primarily local residents, enjoying its unhurried ambiance. Beyond the tranquility lie various beach activities, from the excitement of kayaking, stand-up paddle-boarding, windsurfing, and kitesurfing to the thrill of surfing.

Practicalities such as amenities and facilities are part of the beach experience, ensuring visitors find convenience in their seaside escapades. Directions by car or bus open avenues for exploration, connecting Kailua Bay to Waikiki Beach. Whether opting for a 41-minute bus journey or a scenic 30-minute drive via the Pali Highway, the journey promises a seamless transition from the lively vibes of Waikiki to the relaxed allure of Kailua Bay.

Kayaking Experience

Going on a kayaking journey in Kailua Bay offers an inclusive experience suitable for a range of skill levels, from beginners to seasoned kayakers. It demands a moderate level of fitness and mandates all participants to be proficient swimmers. The essential safety briefing, including instructions on local ocean conditions, underscores the importance of adhering to the provided guidance and utilizing equipment like life jackets and snorkeling gear for a secure and enjoyable outing.

To ensure safety, minimum age and weight restrictions apply, with provisions for children to ride in double kayaks alongside adults. For those seeking independence, Adventure Tours Hawaii extends self-guided kayaking packages, inviting exploration of Kailua Bay, snorkeling at Lanikai, and enjoying picnics on the fossilized reef of Flat Island (Popoi'a). Beginners are encouraged to consider kayaking lessons prior to their Kailua Bay adventure.

Weather Conditions

Remaining attuned to weather conditions is crucial. Checking wind forecasts and understanding current patterns is vital, as strong winds can present challenges during kayaking. Similarly, being mindful of tide information is essential, considering its impact on water levels and access to specific areas. This holistic approach ensures that each kayaking excursion in Kailua Bay is not just an adventure but also a safe and well-prepared exploration.

Permits and Regulations

Before setting off on a kayaking adventure in Kailua Bay, it's essential to navigate the regulatory landscape for a seamless experience. Check for any required permits, particularly if you plan to explore marine protected areas, ensuring compliance with regulations to minimize environmental impact.

Specifically, permits are indispensable for visiting Flat Island or Moku Nui Island (Mokulua Islands), with the Hawaii Department of Land and Natural Resources, Fish and Wildlife Division overseeing these permissions. Commercial operators must hold a valid permit, excluding businesses renting snorkeling and body-boarding equipment. In Waikiki and Kaanapali Ocean Waters, additional permits and requirements are applicable.

Age restrictions play a role in kayak rentals, emphasizing safety and appropriate supervision. For instance, minimum age requirements vary for different tours, with participants under 18 mandated to have adult accompaniment. Island Landing Permits,

integral to kayak rental packages, are included, though it's crucial to note their unavailability on Sundays. Navigating these regulations ensures a responsible and enjoyable kayaking experience in Kailua Bay.

Navigation

Effective navigation is key to a successful kayaking experience in Kailua Bay. Equip yourself with a map of the bay and a compass for reliable navigation tools. Additionally, consider using a waterproof GPS device or a smartphone app with offline maps to enhance your directional awareness.

For those opting for public transportation, buses number 56 or 57 from Ala Moana Shopping Center provide convenient access, with the 56 route taking you close to Kailua town, in proximity to Kailua Bay. If you prefer the flexibility of driving, Kailua Bay is approximately a 40-minute drive from Waikiki Beach. Use a GPS or map application to navigate to Kailua Beach, the starting point for your kayaking adventure.

For kayak rentals and guided tours, Kailua Beach Adventures and Adventure Tours Hawaii are reliable options. Locate their kayak shops at Kailua Beach and check their websites for specific meeting locations, ensuring a smooth and well-guided entry into the stunning waters of Kailua Bay.

Kayak and Equipment

When embarking on a kayaking adventure in Kailua Bay, having the right equipment is crucial. If you don't own a kayak, reliable rental services are available to meet your needs.

Kailua Beach Adventures stands out, offering high-quality kayak rentals and guided tours. They provide all the necessary equipment, including paddles, life jackets, seats, and roof racks. Notably, their commitment to environmental stewardship is reflected in a beach cleanup promotion.

On the other hand, Pat's Kailua specializes in vacation rentals, including beach cottages and homes in the Kailua and Lanikai areas. While they don't specifically offer kayak rentals, their accommodations provide a comfortable base for your Kailua experience.

For those seeking vacation rentals with a wider range of options, VRBO offers houses and cabins in the Kailua Bay area. While not specialized in kayak rentals or guided tours, VRBO provides diverse lodging choices for a memorable stay.

Remember, whether you rent or bring your own, ensure you have a proper paddle and wear a Coast Guard-approved life jacket for a safe and enjoyable kayaking experience in Kailua Bay.

Cost

The cost of kayaking in Kailua Bay varies, offering options to suit different preferences and budgets. When considering your kayaking adventure, several factors influence the overall cost.

Kailua Beach Adventures provides single kayak rentals with flexible durations. For a half-day (4 hours), the price is $69, while a full day costs $84. If you prefer a guided experience, their 2-hour guided kayak excursion is $179 for adults (13+) and $159 for children (8-12).

Adventure Tours Hawaii offers a self-guided kayak tour in Kailua Bay, with fees of $99 for adults (13+) and $89 for children (3-12). Additionally, Viator provides a kayaking tour with lunch, starting from $106.33, allowing you to enjoy the beauty of Kailua Bay with added culinary delights.

For specific tour options and prices, Hawaii Activities is a valuable resource. Ultimately, the diverse range of offerings ensures that you can find a kayaking experience in Kailua Bay that aligns with your preferences and budget.

Safety Precautions

Ensuring a safe and enjoyable kayaking experience in Kailua Bay involves taking essential safety precautions. Understanding and implementing these measures enhances the overall adventure:

- **Emergency Gear:** Prioritize safety gear, including a whistle, first aid kit, and bilge pump. Always wear a life jacket and know how to swim, crucial elements for ocean kayaking safety.

- **Weather and Surf Conditions:** Check the weather forecast and surf report before kayaking. Opt for spots with waves breaking at waist level or below. Leaning back slightly as you paddle over waves helps your kayak navigate smoothly.

- **Area Knowledge:** Familiarize yourself with the area, including directions, start and stop points, weather, and water conditions. Beginners may find reef-protected bays like Kailua Beach ideal for a safe introduction to ocean kayaking.

- **Swimming and Floatation Devices:** Take swimming classes if needed and carry floatation devices. A whistle is essential for communication and safety in case of separation or an unexpected event.

- **Landing Permits and Regulations:** Obtain necessary permits for specific islands, like Flat Island or Moku Nui. Adhering to regulations ensures responsible kayaking practices.

- **Float Plan:** Share your kayaking plans and expected return time with someone trustworthy. This precaution aids in swift response in case of unforeseen circumstances.

- **Communication:** Bring waterproof communication devices, such as a VHF radio or a waterproof phone case, to stay connected and seek assistance if required.

- **Choose a Safe Location:** Select spots with manageable waves. Waiting for a small wave and leaning back during its approach assists in navigating waves safely. These precautions collectively contribute to a secure and memorable kayaking experience.

Wildlife Awareness

Kailua Bay is not just a playground for kayakers but also a haven for diverse marine life. Embracing responsible kayaking involves fostering awareness and respect for the local wildlife.

- **Marine Life:** The bay hosts a rich tapestry of endemic species, from the gentle Hawaiian green sea turtles to nesting seabirds and monk seals. Understanding and respecting their habitat are paramount for a harmonious coexistence.

- **Educate Yourself:** Before embarking on a kayaking journey, educate yourself about the local wildlife and their behaviors. Kailua Beach Adventures offers insightful tours focusing on the bay's unique wildlife, providing valuable knowledge for responsible exploration.

- **Respectful Distance:** When encountering marine life, maintain a respectful distance to prevent disturbance. This ensures minimal impact on their natural behaviors and habitats.

- **Report Injured Wildlife:** In the unfortunate event of encountering entangled or stranded sea turtles or injured marine mammals, such as whales, dolphins, or seals, be proactive. Report these instances to the appropriate authorities, like the NOAA Fisheries Marine Mammal Hotline at 1-888-256-9840, contributing to their protection and well-being. Responsible kayaking entails not only enjoying the beauty of nature but actively participating in its preservation.

Snorkeling Gear

When setting out on a kayaking journey, the possibilities for exploration are not confined to the water's surface alone. Consider enhancing your experience by bringing along snorkeling gear, opening a gateway to the mesmerizing underwater realms.

For a seamless transition between kayaking and snorkeling, ensure you equip yourself with the essentials. A well-fitted diving mask, a reliable pair of fins, and a snorkel form the basic snorkeling gear. Additionally, having a kayak anchor proves beneficial, offering a stable platform for safe and tranquil snorkeling experiences.

Fit is paramount. Ensure your snorkeling gear sits comfortably, allowing unrestricted movement for a safe and enjoyable adventure. Whether kayaking or snorkeling, stay hydrated, dress suitably for the conditions, and, when in doubt, seek guidance from qualified instructors. Unveil the dual wonders of both worlds, above and below the surface, for a holistic and enriching exploration.

Timing

When planning your kayaking expedition in Kailua Bay, timing is key to ensuring a safe and fulfilling experience.

Daylight Hours: Opt for kayaking during daylight hours for enhanced visibility and safety. Mornings are particularly favorable, especially on calm days when the water mirrors the sky, offering crystal-clear views of the vibrant marine life below. The tranquil morning hours provide a smooth journey, setting the stage for an enjoyable outing.

Before going, check the weather forecast and surf report to gauge conditions. This ensures you select the best window for your adventure, maximizing safety and enjoyment.

Some rental services and guided tours offer specific check-in and check-out times, along with flexible schedules to accommodate diverse preferences. Consider these details when planning your excursion to align with your ideal timing.

Wind Conditions: Keep an eye on wind conditions to identify optimal times with calmer winds, enhancing the overall kayaking experience. Timing your adventure thoughtfully ensures a memorable and safe journey through the stunning waters of Kailua Bay.

Physical Preparation

Before embarking on your kayaking journey to Kailua Bay, it's essential to ensure you're physically prepared for the adventure.

Fitness Level: Assess your physical fitness to gauge your ability to handle the duration and intensity of kayaking. While you don't need to be a super athlete, having a moderate level of fitness is important. Kayaking to Kailua Bay requires some effort, so being in relatively good shape and having the ability to swim without a life jacket is advisable.

Hydration and Nutrition: Proper hydration and nutrition are crucial for a successful kayaking expedition.

1. Pack plenty of water and snacks to keep yourself hydrated and energized during the journey. Since you'll be kayaking continuously for several hours, having snacks on hand is essential to sustain your energy levels.

2. Wear lightweight, breathable clothing suitable for the weather to prevent overheating and dehydration. Don't forget to wear a hat and sunglasses to shield yourself from the sun's rays.

3. Drink water regularly throughout the trip to maintain hydration levels. It's important to drink water before you feel thirsty to prevent dehydration.

4. Pack nutritious snacks like fruit, nuts, and energy bars to fuel your body and keep your energy levels up during the kayaking adventure.

By ensuring you're physically prepared with the right fitness level, hydration, and nutrition, you'll be ready to enjoy a rewarding and memorable kayaking experience in Kailua Bay.

Beach Etiquette

When engaging in kayaking activities in the pristine environment of Kailua Bay, observing proper beach etiquette is crucial for preserving the beauty of this natural setting.

One of the fundamental principles of responsible tourism is to leave no trace. Ensure you pick up any trash, including your own, and dispose of it properly. Bring a small bag for your waste and any litter you might find along the way. Minimizing your impact on the environment helps maintain the cleanliness of the beaches and protects the delicate ecosystems surrounding Kailua Bay.

Maintain a respectful distance from marine life, such as Hawaiian green sea turtles, nesting seabirds, and monk seals. Avoid disturbing their natural behaviors and habitats.

If you encounter injured wildlife, report it to the appropriate authorities to ensure timely assistance.

Keep noise levels to a minimum to preserve the tranquility of the bay. Respect the peaceful coexistence of beachgoers and the natural surroundings.

Adhere to local regulations and guidelines to contribute to the preservation of Kailua Bay. Be aware of any restricted areas or specific rules that apply to kayaking in this pristine location.

Carrying a Camera

Carrying a camera on your kayaking adventure can transform your experience into a visual journey, but protecting your gear from water is paramount. Experienced kayakers and photographers offer practical tips for ensuring your camera stays dry and functional throughout the excursion.

Opt for a reliable dry bag to store your camera when not in use. Choose a size that accommodates both the camera and the lens you intend to use. This provides an added layer of protection against splashes and unexpected waves.

For non-waterproof cameras, invest in a waterproof bag or case. While dry cases offer superior protection, they may be less accessible during kayaking. Evaluate the trade-off between protection and ease of access based on your preferences.

Enhance packing efficiency by cutting a round piece for the bag's bottom and a piece encircling its circumference. This facilitates easy packing in kayaks with smaller hatches and ensures convenient access to your camera when needed.

Include a micro-fiber towel in the bag to wipe off incidental water droplets and shield your camera gear from potential bumps during storage. This extra layer safeguards your equipment from both water and physical impacts.

By incorporating these insights, you can capture the beauty of Kailua Bay without compromising the safety of your valuable camera equipment.

Photo Ops While Kayaking Kailua Bay

Planning a kayaking adventure to Kailua Bay opens up a treasure trove of photo opportunities, allowing you to document the beauty and diversity of this Hawaiian paradise.

Kailua Bay and Beach: Begin your photographic journey with the panoramic views of Kailua Bay. The pristine white sand beach, complemented by crystal-clear waters and lush greenery, creates a breathtaking backdrop for memorable photos. Capture the essence of this coastal haven.

Mokulua Islands: Paddle towards the Mokulua Islands and capture the dramatic volcanic landscapes, verdant greenery, and secluded beaches. Each snapshot immortalizes the unique charm and untouched beauty of these islands, leaving you with a visual narrative of your kayaking expedition.

Popoia Island (Flat Island): Venture to Popoia Island, a bird sanctuary. Photograph various bird species dwelling in the sanctuary and explore the fossilized reef, immortalizing the island's geological wonders in your images.

Sea Life: Encounter marine life like Hawaiian green sea turtles, vibrant fish, and playful dolphins. Seize these moments as they unfold, creating a photographic chronicle of your intimate interactions with the underwater world.

Kayaking Adventure: Document your kayaking escapade through Kailua Bay. Capture the rhythmic paddle strokes, the clear waters beneath your kayak, and the camaraderie of fellow adventurers. These images will serve as lasting memories of your remarkable journey.

Segue: In this chapter, we explored the diverse offerings of Kailua Bay, from kayaking to snorkeling, capturing the essence of this Hawaiian gem through practical insights and memorable experiences. As we conclude, remember the importance of preparation, safety, and respect for the environment while embarking on your adventure. Now, prepare to dive into the thrilling world of shark cage diving in the next chapter, where we'll delve into the exhilarating encounters and unforgettable moments awaiting in the depths of the ocean.

Chapter Nine

Sharks - Cage Diving

Don't ask for security, ask for adventure. Better to live 30 years full of adventure than a 100 years safe in the corner. —Jim Rohn

As we plunge into Chapter 9, fasten your seatbelts for an adrenaline-pumping journey into the heart of shark cage diving. Here, readers will discover the thrilling opportunity to witness Galapagos and sandbar sharks in their natural habitat. Guided by reputable operators, we'll explore safety measures, entry techniques, and health considerations, ensuring a secure and educational encounter with these magnificent creatures. From invaluable photography tips to unraveling the socio-economic impact of shark conservation, this chapter promises an unforgettable adventure that goes beyond the surface. Join us as we dive deep into the mesmerizing world of shark cage diving, where excitement and conservation converge.

How to Do

For those seeking the thrill of shark cage diving, there are several reputable operators to consider.

Hawaii Shark Encounters provides tours on the North Shore, offering a blue water experience to observe Galapagos and sandbar sharks. Their educational components underscore the importance of shark conservation.

HawaiiActivities.com also offers tours departing from Haleiwa Harbor, with visitors praising the calmness and curiosity of the sharks.

North Shore Shark Adventures guarantees 100% shark sightings and emphasizes safety and family-friendly tours.

Haleiwa Shark Tours, owned and operated by Native Hawaiians, offers culturally significant encounters, highlighting the sharks' importance in Hawaiian culture and the marine ecosystem.

When choosing an operator, prioritize reputation and certifications to ensure a safe and memorable experience. Look for positive reviews and confirm the operator holds the necessary licenses and certifications for conducting shark cage diving tours.

Cost

Planning the thrilling adventure of shark cage diving in Oahu comes with varying costs based on your chosen tour. Oahu Shark Dive offers an immersive experience at $94.25, providing a chance to witness these magnificent creatures up close. For a price of $135.00, Shark Cage Diving in Oahu promises an exhilarating encounter with sharks beneath the Pacific waters. If you're up for a cage-free experience, Swim with Sharks from Haleiwa is available at $150.00, ensuring a unique and awe-inspiring adventure. North Shore Shark Adventure provides a family-friendly option with rates varying from $80 for child cage divers to $95 for adult cage divers (Kama'aina/Military/Student). For those seeking a cage-free alternative, the Oahu Cage-free Shark Tour is available at $89, offering an unforgettable and budget-friendly shark experience.

Safety Precautions

Choosing a reputable and licensed shark cage diving operator is paramount to ensuring a safe and unforgettable experience. Before the tour, participants undergo a comprehensive safety briefing, acquainting them with rules and precautions aboard the boat. Adhering to these rules, such as remaining still in the water and refraining from sudden movements or touching the sharks or cage, is crucial for safety. Operators provide essential safety equipment like wetsuits, masks, and snorkels to protect divers from the cold water and enable comfortable breathing.

Entering and exiting the cage are carefully managed processes, with divers encouraged to use controlled techniques to minimize risks. It's imperative to stay within the cage and avoid trapping fingers or equipment between the cage bars and the boat. Divers should choose the right exposure suit for the conditions, as cage diving involves extended periods of relative stillness in colder waters.

Thorough safety orientations cover emergency procedures, equipment usage, and exit protocols, ensuring participants are well-prepared for any situation. Prioritizing the condition of equipment, including the shark cage and associated gear, is essential for a safe dive. Whether provided by the operator or brought along, ensuring the availability and quality of wetsuits, masks, and snorkels is vital for a secure and enjoyable experience.

Weather Conditions

Before going on your shark cage diving adventure, it's crucial to check the weather forecast. Unfavorable conditions, such as strong winds or high waves, may lead to cancellations to prioritize safety. Additionally, consider sea conditions, like wave height and current strength, as these factors directly impact the safety and feasibility of the thrilling activity.

Permits and Regulations

Before participating in shark cage diving in Hawaii, it's essential to be aware of specific regulations and permits. According to the Hawaii State Legislature, operators must use shark or diving cages for tours where people enter the water to view sharks. Furthermore, Hawaii's status as the only shark sanctuary in the United States prohibits capturing, entangling, or killing any shark, as mandated by a law passed in 2022. While various operators offer shark cage diving tours in Hawaii, participants must adhere to safety guidelines and instructions provided by the tour companies. It's reassuring that no previous diving experience is required, as skilled divemasters supervise the activity to ensure everyone's safety.

Health Considerations

Before you plan a shark cage diving adventure, it's crucial to consider health factors. Participants should disclose any existing medical conditions to the operator beforehand, especially conditions like heart problems, respiratory disorders, or epilepsy. Consulting with a healthcare provider prior to the dive is essential for individuals with pre-existing medical conditions to ensure their safety.

Additionally, being prepared for potential motion sickness is important. Visitors prone to seasickness should take preventive measures such as medication before the trip to avoid discomfort. It's wise to plan ahead and take necessary precautions to ensure a comfortable and enjoyable experience while shark cage diving. Taking care of one's health and well-being is paramount to fully appreciate and engage in this exhilarating adventure.

Wildlife Education

Shark cage diving extends beyond adventure, providing an opportunity for wildlife education. Before the dive, participants are encouraged to delve into the specifics of the shark species they are likely to encounter. Tour operators often offer educational sessions, sharing valuable insights into shark biology, behavior, and conservation status. These sessions foster a deeper understanding and appreciation for these magnificent creatures.

Participating in shark cage diving can be a positive force for shark conservation. Tour operators follow strict interaction guidelines, emphasizing responsible practices such as avoiding direct contact, not feeding sharks, and using appropriate bait. Beyond the immediate experience, shark cage diving contributes to conservation awareness. Participants are encouraged to become advocates for shark conservation, supporting initiatives and adopting sustainable practices.

Importantly, shark cage diving can have a positive socio-economic impact. It generates revenue for local communities, creates jobs, and supports businesses. By engaging in shark cage diving, participants actively contribute to the preservation of sharks and their habitats while fostering economic growth in local communities.

Photography and Videography

Capturing the mesmerizing moments of shark cage diving requires the right camera equipment. A waterproof camera, particularly a robust GoPro, is essential for preserving underwater footage and photos. These devices, celebrated for their durability and high-quality imaging, ensure that participants can relive the adventure vividly.

For optimal stability and unique angles, a pole or mount becomes a valuable accessory, helping photographers secure stunning shots amidst the underwater spectacle. To safeguard the camera during deeper dives, an underwater housing unit is recommended, offering protection against potential water damage.

Some operators go the extra mile, providing professional photography services that employ DSLR cameras to capture high-resolution images. Additionally, participants can opt for video and photo packages, featuring HD GoPro footage and curated photo highlights of their awe-inspiring shark encounter. These offerings add an extra layer of convenience and expertise to the photography experience, ensuring that every moment is documented with precision and flair.

Timing

Timing is crucial for an unforgettable shark cage diving experience in Oahu. Before diving into the adventure, participants should confirm the duration of their chosen tour and the designated meeting point. In Hawaii, this thrilling activity is available on the North Shore of Oahu, with various operators offering daily tours.

For instance, North Shore Shark Adventures offers a 1.5-hour tour starting at 7 a.m. (or 6 a.m. in June - August), with additional tours scheduled until 11 a.m., depending on availability. One Ocean Divings provides a unique opportunity off the coast of Oahu during the summer through fall months, offering an experience with tiger sharks. Participants must schedule this dive in advance to ensure availability.

Hawaii Shark Encounters offers cage diving at various times throughout the day, providing flexibility for participants to choose a slot that suits their preferences. These carefully scheduled tours ensure that participants can embark on their shark cage diving adventure with confidence and anticipation.

Cancellation Policy

Planning a shark cage diving adventure requires careful consideration of the operator's cancellation policy to ensure a stress-free experience. Each operator in Hawaii may have its own policies, highlighting the importance of understanding the specific procedures. For instance, Hawaii Shark Encounters strictly enforces a no-cancellation or changes policy within 48 hours of the tour, emphasizing the need for participants to commit to their scheduled adventure.

Similarly, Hawaii Adventure Diving allows rescheduling up to 48 hours before the tour, providing flexibility for participants to adjust their plans based on availability. In the case of inclement weather, this operator offers the option to reschedule or provides a full refund, demonstrating a customer-centric approach.

North Shore Shark Adventures requires cancellations or changes to be made at least 24 hours before the scheduled tour, providing participants with a reasonable timeframe to make adjustments if needed. Understanding and adhering to these policies contribute to a smoother and more enjoyable shark cage diving experience.

Group Size

Understanding the group dynamics and post-dive debriefing is crucial for a fulfilling shark cage diving experience. The cage capacity varies among operators, impacting the number of participants in the water simultaneously. Great White Shark Tours, for instance, accommodates up to 8 divers in their 4.2-meter-long cage, ensuring a collective yet personalized encounter with sharks. White Shark Projects, with a custom-built catamaran, limits capacity to 20 passengers and 5 crew members, prioritizing a comfortable and safe environment.

Adrenaline's Shark Diving Oahu considers factors like passenger count, size, and ability, allowing up to 7 people in the cage comfortably. This tailored approach ensures that participants can fully immerse themselves in the experience while adhering to safety standards.

Post-dive debriefing sessions play a pivotal role in enhancing the overall shark cage diving experience. These sessions cover various aspects, starting with safety protocols. Operators, such as those in Hawaii, emphasize the use of sturdy cages, experienced divemasters, and strict safety guidelines to ensure participant well-being.

The debriefing also delves into shark behavior, debunking misconceptions and highlighting the sharks' calm demeanor and curiosity towards divers. This educational component fosters a deeper understanding and appreciation for these incredible marine creatures.

Conservation efforts take center stage in the debriefing, underscoring how shark cage diving contributes to these initiatives. Operators often share their involvement in local conservation projects, fostering a sense of responsibility among participants towards marine life protection.

Participants' feedback becomes a valuable part of the debriefing, creating a sense of camaraderie and shared experiences. The opportunity for individuals to express their thoughts, feelings, and insights further enriches the collective journey.

The debriefing session extends beyond the immediate experience, informing participants about future opportunities in shark cage diving or other marine conservation efforts. This encouragement ensures that participants remain engaged with marine life conservation beyond their initial adventure.

In essence, the post-dive debriefing is not just a conclusion to the day's activities; it serves as a bridge between the immediate experience and a sustained commitment to marine conservation, fostering a community of informed and passionate advocates for the ocean's well-being.

Segue: As we conclude our adrenaline-pumping journey into the mesmerizing realm of shark cage diving, we've delved into an unparalleled adventure where the enigmatic Galapagos and sandbar sharks become our co-stars. From safety measures and entry techniques to the socio-economic impact of shark conservation, this chapter has unraveled the intricacies of an unforgettable underwater experience.

Key takeaways echo the importance of choosing reputable operators, understanding safety measures, and embracing the educational facets of shark encounters. We've debunked myths, celebrated conservation efforts, and shared in the awe of sharks' calm curiosity.

Yet, our quest for thrills and exploration doesn't end here. Brace yourself for the next chapter, where we'll soar to new heights – both literally and figuratively. Our focus shifts to the exhilarating world of ziplining, promising an adrenaline rush amidst stunning landscapes. From safety harnesses to panoramic views, get ready to elevate your adventure.

Remember, the journey is not just about conquering fears but embracing the uncharted territories of our own courage. So, fasten your seatbelts; the zipline awaits to carry us into the skies, and the unknown beckons us once again. Adventure never rests, and neither do we.

Chapter Ten

Kualoa Ranch

Why do you go away? So that you can come back. So that you can see the place you came from with new eyes and extra colors. And the people there see you differently, too. Coming back to where you started is not the same as never leaving. —Terry Pratchett

As we begin a new chapter, we return to the roots of adventure at Kualoa Ranch, exploring the exhilarating world of ziplining. Just as Terry Pratchett beautifully captures the essence of returning, we invite you to rediscover the familiar with a renewed perspective.

In this chapter, we unravel the essentials of ziplining, focusing on safety, enjoyment, and the breathtaking landscapes of Kualoa Ranch. Dive into the significance of safety equipment, the training of operators, and the crucial role reputable operators play in enhancing your experience.

Discover the highlights of ziplining experiences in Hawaii, particularly at Kualoa Ranch, where each zip offers not just an adrenaline rush but a journey through the lush and vibrant landscapes. We'll delve into tour highlights, safety measures, health restrictions, and the recommended attire for a seamless and thrilling adventure.

But the excitement doesn't end there. Our exploration extends to the diverse activities at Kualoa Ranch, promising a comprehensive guide for an unforgettable adventure. So, let's soar through the skies, embrace the thrill, and rediscover the beauty of Kualoa Ranch with a fresh set of eyes. The adventure continues, and the ranch beckons us to new heights!

About Ziplining

Going on a ziplining adventure at Kualoa Ranch demands more than just a sense of thrill—it requires a commitment to safety. As riders prepare to take flight, they gear up with essential safety equipment. A snug-fitting helmet rests securely on their heads, a harness ensures a firm connection to the zipline, and gloves provide a comfortable grip, turning each descent into a controlled, exhilarating journey.

Behind every zip, the unsung heroes are the operators—individuals trained meticulously in zipline operations and safety protocols. Their expertise is the backbone of a secure and enjoyable experience. Participants find reassurance in the knowledge that their guides are not just thrill-seekers but professionals dedicated to ensuring the safety of every rider.

While the allure of ziplining is undeniable, the primary risks lie in user errors. This isn't just about soaring through the air; it's about attentiveness and adherence to guidelines. The zipline operator's instructions become a lifeline, a crucial element that separates a breathtaking descent from an unsafe one.

Choosing a zipline operator with an impeccable safety record becomes paramount. Reputable operators, adorned with positive reviews, stand as gatekeepers of secure adventures. As riders trust their safety to these operators, they forge a partnership that transcends the bounds of gravity.

Zooming through the skies isn't just about individual thrills—it's about entrusting oneself to the hands of experts. The zipline's design, engineering, and construction play pivotal roles. Commercial ziplines boast comprehensive electro-mechanical systems and sophisticated braking mechanisms. The machinery, the cables, and the platforms are more than components—they are the guardians of a seamless flight.

In the realm of ziplining, safety is not an afterthought; it's an integral part of the experience. It's the unspoken pact between the riders, the operators, and the zipline itself—a commitment to turn every descent into an adventure where exhilaration and safety dance in harmony.

Ziplining Experiences in Hawaii

In the tropical embrace of Hawaii, ziplining takes adventure seekers on an unforgettable journey, weaving through lush landscapes and over breathtaking vistas. Kohala Zipline, nestled in Hālawa, invites participants to a three-hour escapade, blending ziplining thrills with a scenic hike, a delectable lunch, and a refreshing dip beneath a private waterfall. It's not just an adventure; it's a sensory immersion into Hawaii's natural wonders.

Umauma Falls Zipline and Rappel Experience elevates the excitement, offering a heart-pounding ride over 14 mesmerizing waterfalls, coupled with the thrill of rappelling. The rush of wind and the roar of water create a symphony of exhilaration that resonates with every plunge.

Kualoa Ranch beckons with its Jurassic Valley Zipline Tour, a captivating journey through Ka'a'awa Valley. Suspended over lush landscapes, participants traverse suspension bridges and explore short hiking nature trails, experiencing the thrill of ziplines ranging from 200 feet to a quarter of a mile in length. It's not just ziplining; it's a cinematic adventure in the heart of Jurassic landscapes.

For those seeking Maui's zipline embrace, Maui Zipline Company offers a centrally located experience, while Jungle Zipline Maui and Pi'iholo Ranch Zipline combine zipping with invigorating hikes, creating an immersive connection with Maui's diverse terrain.

The Big Island Zipline Adventure, set against the backdrop of Kolekole Falls, boasts seven awe-inspiring lines, stitching together an adventure quilt with panoramic ocean views. In the realm of Hawaiian ziplining, it's not just about the adrenaline; it's about surrendering to the island's embrace, allowing every zipline to become a brushstroke on the canvas of an unforgettable Hawaiian adventure.

About Kualoa Ranch

Nestled atop the Ka'a'awa Valley, Kualoa Ranch sets the stage for an exhilarating ziplining escapade, inviting participants to immerse themselves in stunning views and an unforgettable adventure. With seven tandem sections, friends and couples can share the thrill, traversing the valley's expanse side by side. The experience extends beyond ziplining, featuring two suspension bridges and three hiking mini-trails that delve into the valley's rich cultural history and Hawaiian traditions. It's not just a zipline tour; it's a cultural odyssey through the heart of Hawaii.

Safety and fun intertwine seamlessly in the design of the zipline tour, boasting a state-of-the-art automatic braking system. This not only ensures a secure experience but also makes it accessible for individuals without previous ziplining experience. Trained guides accompany participants throughout the 2.5-hour adventure, managing safety equipment and curating an atmosphere where every moment is memorable and secure.

The cost of the Jurassic Valley Zipline Tour at Kualoa Ranch stands at $174.95 per adult, plus 4.712% tax. Additional tour packages, such as the 7-Line Dual Zipline, are priced at $183.00 per adult and $147.00 per child (ages 10-12). Across Oahu, zipline tours can range from $150 to $200, influenced by location, tour length, and add-ons. For the most up-to-date pricing and availability, checking with the respective companies is always advisable.

Guests are advised to be in moderately good shape, capable of navigating varied and rugged terrain. Specific health conditions, such as heart issues or joint pain, warrant consultation with a doctor before participating. Pregnant women are discouraged from taking part in the zipline tour.

Attire plays a pivotal role in ensuring a comfortable experience, with closed-toed footwear featuring a closed heel or heel strap as a requirement. The recommended comfortable clothing allows for freedom of movement, enhancing the overall enjoyment of the adventure.

For those journeying from Waikiki Beach to Kualoa Ranch, options include taking two buses (#2 and #60) for a 1-hour and 45-minute commute or opting for a transfer service with Paradise Hawaii Tours, which takes approximately 45 minutes with light traffic. Kualoa Ranch also offers transportation for select tours at an additional fee of $30 per person plus tax, with pickup locations at Fin Waikiki Hotel, Sheraton Waikiki Hotel, and The Hilton Hawaiian Village for early or mid-morning pickups.

Other Activities at Kualoa Ranch

Beyond the thrilling zipline adventure, Kualoa Ranch unfolds a tapestry of diverse activities, ensuring visitors a kaleidoscopic experience in the heart of Hawaii.

The *Movie Sites and Ranch Tour* traverses the iconic Ka'a'awa Valley, a cinematic haven where over 200 Hollywood movies and television shows have left their indelible mark. It's a cinematic pilgrimage through breathtaking landscapes that have played starring roles in some of the world's most beloved films.

Embarking on the *Kualoa Grown Tour*, guests hop on an open-air trolley, immersing themselves in Kualoa's farming operations. The tour unfolds the story of tropical fruit and flower gardens, and an ancient fishpond, offering insights into the ranch's rich agricultural heritage.

For those seeking the crème de la crème, the *Best of Kualoa Experience Package* is a treasure trove. This comprehensive package encompasses three 90-minute Hawaiian experience tours – the Hollywood Movie Sites Tour, the Jurassic Jungle Expedition, and the Kualoa Grown Tour. To crown it all, a free all-you-can-eat buffet lunch awaits, providing a feast for both the senses and the palate.

The *UTV Raptor Tours* elevate the adventure, allowing participants to explore the remote corners of Kaaawa's "Jurassic" Valley. These multi-passenger UTV Raptor vehicles promise an immersive journey through lush landscapes, creating an indomitable memory.

Opting for the *2-Hour Ride-Along UTV Raptor Tour* introduces a unique twist. Passengers can now entrust the exploration to a professional guide, freeing them to soak in the beauty of Kualoa without the need to navigate.

For a fusion of nature and technology, the *Electric Mountain Bike Tour* offers an eco-friendly exploration of Kualoa. On pedal-assisted electric mountain bikes, visitors ride through the ranch under the guidance of a knowledgeable tour guide, enjoying a thrilling and environmentally conscious adventure.

The *2-Hour Horseback Walking Tour* opens a portal to a bygone era, allowing guests to meander through the scenic wonders of Kualoa Ranch on horseback. It's a timeless experience, blending tradition with the enchanting beauty of the surroundings.

Kualoa Ranch stands not merely as a ziplining haven but as a multi-faceted gem, beckoning adventurers to explore the diverse offerings that paint a vivid portrait of Hawaii's cultural, cinematic, and natural wonders.

Segue: As we soar through the exhilarating world of ziplining at Kualoa Ranch, safety and enjoyment intertwine in a dance of adventure. From the rush of the zipline to the lush landscapes that echo cinematic history, Kualoa offers a symphony of experiences. As we bid adieu to the zipline's thrill, our next stop invites you to delve into the cultural heartbeat of Hawaii. Uncover the traditions, stories, and vibrant heritage that breathe life into the islands in our upcoming chapter on cultural activities. Get ready to immerse yourself in the soul-stirring rhythms of Hawaii's rich cultural tapestry.

Chapter Eleven

Exploring Oahu's Culture and History

Mālama i ka 'āina, e ola mau ai. —Take care of the land, and it will take care of you. —Hawaiian proverb.

L et's go on a cultural odyssey through the pages of history as we unfold the vibrant hues of Hawaii in this chapter. Begin at the hallowed grounds of Pearl Harbor National Memorial, where echoes of the past resonate. Immerse yourself in the living legacy of Polynesia at the Polynesian Cultural Center, a kaleidoscope of immersive experiences. Journey through time at Iolani Palace, where royal history whispers tales of a bygone era.

But our exploration doesn't stop there. Dive into the heart of Hawaiian culture through its culinary delights – from traditional feasts to the flavors of food trucks. Feel the warm embrace of a Hawaiian sunset on a romantic dinner cruise, where the sea mirrors the sky's vibrant hues.

As we traverse Oahu's cultural landscape, remember the wisdom of the Hawaiian proverb – take care of the land, and it will take care of you. Let this chapter be a celebration of Hawaii's rich culture, inviting you to savor its essence and allure. Join us as we unveil the treasures that make Oahu a living testament to history, culture, and the enduring spirit of the islands.

Pearl Harbor and USS Arizona Memorial

Discover the solemn echoes of history at the Pearl Harbor National Memorial and the USS Arizona Memorial, where the Pacific theater of World War II unfolds in a poignant narrative of sacrifice and remembrance.

Historical Significance

Immersed in the heart of Joint Base Pearl Harbor-Hickam, the Pearl Harbor National Memorial, and its partners serve as custodians of World War II history in the Pacific. It is a poignant tribute, preserving and interpreting the events that led to the infamous December 7, 1941, attack on Oahu. The memorial comprises nine historic sites, each weaving a different facet of the war's narrative. Among them, the USS Arizona Memorial stands as a sacred ground, marking the resting place of 1,102 souls who perished on the USS Arizona (USS Arizona Memorial Tour, 2011).

Visitor Information and Tips

The memorial, a testament to valor and sacrifice, opens its doors daily from 7 a.m. to 5 p.m., with the exception of Christmas Day. Visitors embark on a boat ride from the Pearl

Harbor Visitor Center to access the USS Arizona Memorial. While the memorial itself is free, reservations are recommended for the National Park Service facilitated USS Arizona Memorial, ensuring a seamless and meaningful visit.

Beyond the historical pilgrimage, visitors are invited to partake in enriching activities, immersing themselves in the vibrant Hawaiian culture. From harvesting kalo (taro) in traditional lo'i to lei-making, lauhala weaving, 'ukulele lessons, and hula sessions, the experience extends beyond the historical to embrace the living culture of Hawaii (USS Arizona Memorial Tour, 2011).

How to Reach from Waikiki Beach

Going on this historical journey from the lively shores of Waikiki Beach offers multiple avenues. The #20 or #42 public bus (TheBus) provides a scenic route, taking approximately over an hour, allowing visitors to soak in the island's beauty. For those seeking a more direct route, shuttle services and tour packages with round-trip transportation offer convenience and local insights.

Driving enthusiasts can navigate the bustling metropolis of Honolulu, with the trip generally taking 45 minutes by car. Clear directions provided by the Pearl Harbor National Memorial guide the way, ensuring a seamless journey to 1 Arizona Memorial Place, Honolulu, Hawaii 96818.

Cost

While the entry to the Pearl Harbor National Memorial, including the USS Arizona Memorial, is free, a symbolic $1 service charge collected by recreation.gov secures reservations for the USS Arizona Memorial. This nominal fee reflects a commitment to preserving the memorial's integrity and facilitating a thoughtful and secure visit.

In the sacred waters of Pearl Harbor, the USS Arizona Memorial stands as a testament to the courage of those who gave their all. This chapter invites you to tread softly on this hallowed ground, embracing the poignant legacy of Pearl Harbor and honoring the spirit of resilience that defines Hawaii.

Polynesian Cultural Center

Immerse yourself in the vibrant colors of Polynesia at the Polynesian Cultural Center, where the spirit of the islands comes to life through immersive cultural experiences and captivating performances.

Historical Significance

Nestled on 42 acres along Oahu's North Shore, the Polynesian Cultural Center serves as a living museum, preserving the diverse cultures of the Pacific. With its six Polynesian villages, luau, and evening show, it offers visitors a glimpse into the rich heritage of several Polynesian islands (Polynesian Cultural Center, 2022). From the ancient customs of Fiji to the mesmerizing dances of Tahiti, each village showcases the unique traditions and lifestyles of its people.

Visitor Information

As Hawaii's top visitor attraction, the center opens its doors daily, inviting guests to embark on a cultural journey like no other. Visitors can engage in hands-on activities, explore beautifully landscaped gardens, and savor a dinner buffet featuring traditional Polynesian dishes. The highlight of the evening is the spectacular "Hā: Breath of Life" show, where traditional dances and music from across the Pacific come to life with stunning visual effects.

Cost

The Polynesian Cultural Center offers various package options catering to different preferences. From basic same-day admission to full-day packages with transportation included, there's an option for every traveler. Prices range from $64.95 for adult admission to $270.00 for full-day tours from Waikiki hotels, ensuring accessibility for all visitors.

How to Reach From Waikiki Beach

Traveling to the Polynesian Cultural Center is convenient, with options ranging from bus rides to shuttle services. Visitors can take a scenic two-hour bus ride from Waikiki or opt for the center's shuttle service, which can be booked along with tickets. Complimentary parking is also available for those traveling by car, ensuring a hassle-free arrival.

For those opting for public transportation, a bus ride presents a scenic route, with the journey taking approximately 2 hours. The cost is an affordable $5 for a round trip per person, with variations based on your specific location in Waikiki. This mode of travel offers not just a means of transportation but also an opportunity to soak in the island's beauty as you make your way to the center.

Taxis provide a more personalized travel experience, offering convenience and a quicker journey to the Polynesian Cultural Center. If you prefer the autonomy of driving, you can take to the roads and embrace the freedom to explore at your own pace.

For a hassle-free and curated experience, the Polynesian Cultural Center provides a dedicated shuttle service. This service can be conveniently bundled with your tickets or booked separately by reaching out to their Reservation Center at 800-367-7060. The shuttle ensures a seamless transition from your starting point to the heart of Polynesia, allowing you to focus on the anticipation of the cultural exploration awaiting you.

For those who relish the freedom of the open road, driving to the Polynesian Cultural Center is a viable option. Allowing yourself a comfortable window of 60-75 minutes for the journey, the drive provides the flexibility to stop and admire the scenic landscapes along the way. The center's address, 55-370 Kamehameha Hwy, Laie, HI 96762, serves as a beacon guiding you to your destination.

Immersive Cultural Experiences

At the Polynesian Cultural Center, visitors are invited to engage in a plethora of immersive cultural experiences. From participating in hands-on activities like coconut husking and firestarting to exploring native villages and learning about traditional crafts, there's something for everyone to enjoy. The Hawaiian Journey Theater offers a cinematic experience like no other, transporting guests into the heart of Hawaii's rich history and connection to the land.

Luau Tradition

No visit to the Polynesian Cultural Center is complete without experiencing the authentic Hawaiian luau tradition. More than just a feast, the luau represents the essence of Hawaiian culture, with each detail infused with significance and meaning. From the rhythmic beats of the drums to the savory flavors of traditional dishes like kalua pig and poi, every aspect of the luau celebrates the spirit of aloha.

Iolani Palace: Royal History in the Heart of Honolulu

Nestled in the heart of downtown Honolulu, Iolani Palace stands as a testament to Hawaii's royal legacy. Built in 1882 by King Kalakaua, this National Historic Landmark served as the official royal residence and the epicenter of the Kingdom's political and social life until the monarchy's overthrow in 1893. The palace resonates with the echoes of grandeur, having been the venue for official functions, diplomatic receptions, and lavish entertainments hosted by Hawaiian monarchs. Today, it opens its doors to the public, inviting them to explore the first-floor reception areas and the second-floor private suites, delving into the rich history and cultural significance that define the spirit of Hawaii.

How to Reach from Waikiki Beach

For those eager to delve into Hawaii's royal history, reaching Iolani Palace from Waikiki Beach offers multiple avenues. Whether opting for a bus, taxi, or a leisurely walk, each mode of transport unveils a different facet of Oahu's charm. The bus ride, taking approximately 11-15 minutes, provides a window into the diverse landscapes leading to downtown Honolulu. For those seeking a more personal journey, taxis or a scenic stroll present enticing alternatives. The palace's address, 364 South King Street, Honolulu, HI 96813, serves as a beacon, guiding visitors to this historical gem.

Palace Tour Details

Iolani Palace beckons with various tour options, ensuring a nuanced exploration of its history and architectural splendor. Guided tours, led by knowledgeable palace docents, offer immersive insights into the first and second floors. Alternatively, self-led audio tours provide a personalized experience, allowing visitors to meander through the palace at their own pace. The White Glove Tour, a specialty offering on Thursdays, delves deeper into the treasures of the Throne Room, State Dining Room, and King Kalakaua's Library. This intimate 90-minute experience, led by the palace historian, unveils the meticulous care dedicated to preserving cultural legacies.

Entry Fees

The palace extends a warm invitation to all, with entry fees catering to different categories of visitors. General admission rates, kamaaina discounts for Hawaii residents, and military admission options ensure accessibility. The Kalakaua Legacy Tour, a special offering, immerses guests in an extended exploration of the palace's historical nuances. Complimentary tickets on Kamaaina Sundays foster a sense of community engagement, making the palace a welcoming space for all.

Preservation Efforts

Preserving Iolani Palace is a labor of love undertaken by The Friends of Iolani Palace, a non-profit organization dedicated to safeguarding this historic site. Their commitment extends beyond mere conservation, encompassing restoration projects, educational initiatives, and the protection of Iolani Palace's legacy. The organization's involvement in conservation treatments, restoration projects, and education programs ensures that the palace remains a living, breathing testament to Hawaii's past and future.

The ongoing restoration efforts, supported by grants and donations, reflect a collective dedication to maintaining Iolani Palace's cultural significance. As the palace receives funds from initiatives like the Save America's Treasures grant program, it reinforces the commitment to preserving this iconic landmark for generations to come.

In exploring Iolani Palace, visitors go on a journey through time, connecting with Hawaii's royal heritage in a way that transcends the pages of history books. As the palace stands resilient against the passage of time, it continues to be a beacon, inviting all to witness and cherish the rich tapestry of Hawaii's cultural identity.

Traditional Hawaiian Cuisine

Dining in Hawaii is more than a culinary experience; it's a journey through the vibrant history and diverse culture of the islands. Traditional Hawaiian cuisine, a fusion of Polynesian, Asian, and Western influences, offers a delectable tapestry of flavors and techniques. It's a reflection of the rich heritage that has shaped the Hawaiian Islands into a gastronomic paradise.

Here are some must-try dishes:

- **Poi:** Poi, a staple in Hawaiian cuisine, emerges from the taro plant's underground stem. Cooked and pounded into a smooth, starchy paste, poi holds a special place in Hawaiian meals. Its earthy taste and unique texture make it a culinary emblem, connecting diners to the islands' roots.

- **Laulau:** Immerse yourself in the flavors of laulau, a traditional Hawaiian dish that wraps pork, fish, or chicken in taro leaves. Steamed until tender, laulau showcases the islands' bounty, blending savory meats with the subtle sweetness of taro leaves.

- **Kalua Pig:** The aroma of slow-cooked Kalua Pig, prepared in an underground oven called an "imu," wafts through Hawaiian gatherings. The result is tender, flavorful meat that epitomizes the artistry of traditional Hawaiian cooking.

- **Poke:** For seafood enthusiasts, poke is a must-try delicacy. This dish features cubed, raw fish—often ahi tuna—seasoned with soy sauce, sesame oil, seaweed, and chili peppers. Its freshness encapsulates the essence of Hawaii's coastal abundance.

- **Lomi Lomi Salmon:** Celebrations in Hawaii are incomplete without Lomi Lomi Salmon. This side dish, comprised of salted salmon, tomatoes, onions, and chili peppers, adds a burst of flavors to luaus and festive occasions, embodying the spirit of communal feasting.

- **Haupia:** Sweet endings find their pinnacle in Haupia, a coconut milk-based dessert with a velvety texture akin to pudding. Served at Hawaiian gatherings and celebrations, Haupia's creamy indulgence encapsulates the sweetness of Hawaiian hospitality.

- **Saimin:** A noodle soup with roots in Japanese, Chinese, and Filipino cuisines, Saimin showcases Hawaii's multicultural influences. Egg noodles swim in a clear broth, offering a comforting and flavorful experience enhanced by various toppings.

Venturing beyond the tourist-centric eateries allows for authentic encounters with Hawaiian cuisine. Locals often recommend neighborhood spots, food trucks, and farmers' markets where traditional dishes are prepared with love and authenticity.

Local Food Markets and Eateries

Upon landing at Hilo International Airport, the vibrant Hilo Farmers Market becomes a welcoming introduction to the island's flavors. Open daily, the market transforms into a bustling hub on Wednesdays and Saturdays, boasting over 200 vendors offering a myriad of delights—from locally grown macadamia nuts to vibrant handcrafted Hawaiian-style clothes and art. The air is filled with the sweet fragrance of papayas, and the spirit of aloha permeates the lively market.

Heading north of Hilo, Hamakua Harvest, held on Sundays, offers a picturesque setting overlooking the ocean. Here, visitors can relish fresh produce, artisan bread, local honey, and the enticing aroma of smoked fish. Waimea Town Market, situated between Hamakua and Kona, captivates on Saturdays, where a diverse array of vendors caters to every culinary desire. From locally grown coffee beans to goat cheese and gourmet chocolate, the market epitomizes the richness of Hawaii's agriculture.

In Kona, the Saturday Keauhou Farmers Market exclusively features products grown on Hawaii Island, while the Sunday Pure Kona Green Market proudly showcases items made in Kona. Both markets celebrate the essence of local produce, fostering a deep connection between farmers and consumers.

For visitors staying in Waikiki, Mahiku Farmers Market at Hyatt Regency Waikiki Beach Resort and Spa, and International Market Place offers farm-fresh food on Mondays, Wednesdays, and Thursdays. Kapiolani Community College Farmers Market near Diamond Head, a local favorite on Saturdays, features renowned restaurants like The Pig and The Lady, creating a vibrant culinary atmosphere. Kakaako Farmers Market at Ward Village dazzles on Saturdays, with 120 talented vendors lining Ala Moana Boulevard. The Honolulu Farmers Market at Neal S. Blaisdell Center on Wednesday afternoons and Kailua Farmers Market on Thursday afternoons offer exciting alternatives for those who prefer a later start.

Food Truck Frenzy

Going on a culinary journey across Oahu wouldn't be complete without indulging in the diverse offerings of the island's vibrant food trucks. Oahu, boasting the highest number of food trucks among the Hawaiian islands, promises a delightful experience for food enthusiasts seeking a taste of local treasures.

- **Giovanni's Shrimp Truck:** An icon on the North Shore, Giovanni's Shrimp Truck stands as one of the oldest and most beloved food trucks. With outposts in Kahuku, Hale'iwa, and Honolulu, it tempts taste buds with a selection of over 10 shrimp plates. From the signature garlic shrimp to the hot and spicy or coconut-infused varieties, each dish is a testament to Giovanni's enduring popularity.

- **Mike's Huli Chicken:** For aficionados of Hawaiian-style barbecued chicken, Mike's Huli Chicken is a haven. Cooked over kiawe wood, flavored with Hawaiian sea salt, and accompanied by a sweet, tangy, and spicy sauce, every bite is a celebration of island flavors. The sheltered patio provides a relaxed setting to savor this mouthwatering experience.

- **Sunrise Shack:** Born on a plumeria farm in Sunset Beach, Sunrise Shack radiates sunshine with its buttercup yellow charm. From Hale'iwa to Waikiki, it entices with excellent acai bowls, flavorful coffee, invigorating smoothies, and even a touch of home with avocado on toast. Founded by local surfers, it embodies the spirit of the Hawaiian shores.

- **Hale'iwa Bowls:** A haven for the health-conscious, Hale'iwa Bowls elevates the acai experience with nutrient-packed toppings. Beyond acai bowls, indulge in refreshing smoothies and vibrant fruit and vegetable juices, a perfect pitstop for those seeking a nutritious and delicious treat.

- **Elena's Lunchwagon:** Expanding from the original Filipino restaurant, Elena's Lunchwagon graces Downtown Honolulu with culinary delights. Indulge in pork adobo fried rice omelettes, crispy lechon special, and sautéed squid, a testament to the delectable fusion of traditional Filipino flavors.

- **Five Star Poke:** True to its name, Five Star Poke stands as the go-to spot for poke bowls in Honolulu. Featuring flavors like garlic shoyu ahi tuna, jalapeno salmon, and sesame mayo shrimp, each bowl is a burst of freshness. Opt for the optional guacamole topping to elevate your poke experience.

Sunset Dinner Cruises

Pacific Star Sunset Buffet & Show Cruise: Go on an enchanting journey aboard the Pacific Star Sunset Buffet & Show Cruise, where the warm embrace of Aloha awaits. Sip on a refreshing Mai Tai as you're welcomed aboard, setting the tone for an unforgettable evening. Indulge in a delectable Pacific Rim dinner buffet featuring a mouthwatering roast beef carving station amidst stunning coastal views as the sun dips below the horizon.

Star Casual Sunset Dinner & Show: Step into a world of leisure and relaxation with the Star Casual Sunset Dinner & Show, where Friday evenings transform into magical moments. Savor a sumptuous feast featuring crab, tenderloin of beef, and BBQ chicken, complemented by panoramic views of the Hawaiian sunset from four expansive decks. As the evening unfolds, immerse yourself in the captivating "65 Years of Aloha" show, igniting the dance floor with joyous rhythms and melodies.

Historical Dinner Cruise to Kealakekua Bay: Embark on a captivating journey through Hawaii's rich history aboard the Historical Dinner Cruise to Kealakekua Bay. Glide along the Kona Coast, guided by a knowledgeable local historian who unveils over 50 points of interest and historic sites along the way. Discover the legacy of Captain Cook's monument as you sail 12 miles down the coast, enveloped in the tranquil beauty of the Pacific Ocean at sunset.

Segue: As we conclude this chapter delving into Oahu's vibrant tapestry, we've explored the historical echoes at Pearl Harbor, danced through Polynesian cultures, ventured into royal history at Iolani Palace, savored traditional Hawaiian cuisine, wandered local markets, indulged in food truck delights, and sailed into the sunset on enchanting dinner cruises. The key takeaway echoes the Hawaiian proverb, "Mālama i ka ʻāina, e ola mau ai" – Take care of the land, and it will take care of you.

Chapter Twelve

Mahalo

As we close the final page of this book, I want to express my deepest gratitude for joining me on this remarkable journey through the heart and soul of this enchanting island. Oahu, with its rich tapestry of culture, breathtaking landscapes, and thrilling adventures, is not just a destination—it's an experience that leaves an indelible mark on your soul.

Throughout our exploration, we've delved into Oahu's unique blend of tradition and modernity, surfed the azure waves, hiked the verdant trails, and savored the diverse flavors that make Oahu's cuisine a true delight. It's more than just a guide; it's a companion that has been by your side, helping you uncover the island's secrets and guiding you toward authentic experiences that transcend the typical tourist trail.

At its core, this book is a celebration of the Aloha spirit that permeates every corner of this island. It's a reminder that beyond the bustling city life and the sun-kissed beaches, there's a deeper connection waiting to be forged with the land and its people. The Aloha spirit isn't just a greeting; it's a way of life that encourages love, compassion, and respect—a spirit that has touched your journey.

In the midst of the challenges and pain points travelers face, whether it's feeling disconnected or overwhelmed by choices, this book aims to be your reliable companion, offering solutions and shortcuts. It understands the frustrations of missing out on authentic experiences, the anxiety of decision fatigue, and the guilt associated with environmental impact.

We addressed the time constraints that often hinder thorough research, the fear of missing out on hidden gems, and the financial constraints that may limit the spectrum of experiences. Safety concerns, the struggle to navigate local customs, and the difficulty of capturing and reliving memories were all recognized and addressed, making this guide a comprehensive and empathetic resource.

The catalyst that brought you to "Adventuring Oahu" might have been a desire for a deeper connection, an escape from decision fatigue, or the need for an environmentally conscious guide. Whatever the trigger, this book was crafted to be your ally, understanding your needs and providing a roadmap for an unfor-gettable Oahu adventure.

As you reflect on the pages turned and the adventures embraced, remember that Oahu's story doesn't end here. It continues with each traveler who treads upon its shores, leaving their own footprints in the sands of history. As you carry the memories of this journey, may the spirit of Aloha accompany you, inspiring kindness, joy, and a sense of wonder wherever you go.

From the captivating sunsets to the lush valleys, from the rhythmic hula dances to the crashing waves, Oahu has woven its magic into your story. It's a tale of exploration, discovery, and the enduring spirit of Aloha that transcends time and space.

As we draw the final curtain on this adventure, I want to leave you with more than just memories; I want to leave you with an invitation. Your Oahu adventure doesn't end here; it's just beginning. The lush landscapes, vibrant culture, and endless possibilities await your footsteps.

Embark on your Oahu adventure now! Turn these pages into memories. Plan, explore, and savor the magic of Hawaii. Don't miss out on the thrill. Click "Add to Cart" and let your Oahu escapade unfold. Your journey starts with a simple action: grab your guide and immerse yourself in the aloha spirit!

I hope this guide has been your compass, steering you toward authentic experiences, unveiling hidden gems, and fostering a deep connection with Oahu. As you navigate the bustling streets of Honolulu or find serenity on the North Shore, may these pages be your trusted companion.

On a personal note, I want to express my sincere gratitude for choosing this book. Your trust in this guide means the world, and I genuinely hope it has enriched your journey.

If you've enjoyed the adventure, I'd love to hear about it. Your reviews and feedback are the lifeblood of authors, guiding future travelers on their own quests. So, take a moment to share your thoughts. Your words may inspire the next adventurer to explore Oahu with the same enthusiasm and wonder.

I wish you countless more adventures, breathtaking sunsets, and the warm embrace of the Aloha spirit. Until we meet again, whether in the pages of another guide or under the Oahu sun, safe travels and mahalo!

Aloha, Adventurers!

I hope you've enjoyed your journey through the Oahu Travel and Adventure Guide. As the author of this book, I am deeply passionate about sharing the wonders of Hawaii with adventurers like yourself.

Your experience with the guide is invaluable to me. Your honest feedback can help me improve future editions and ensure that every traveler who picks up this book has the best possible experience exploring Oahu.

If you have a few moments to spare, I would be incredibly grateful if you could leave a review sharing your thoughts on the guide. Your review doesn't have to be lengthy or elaborate—just a few words about what you liked or how the guide helped you would mean the world to me.

Your support and feedback mean everything as I continue on this journey of sharing the magic of Hawaii with the world. Mahalo nui loa for your time and consideration.

With warmest aloha, Ocean Breeze Adventures

Keep an eye out for our next adventure, MAUI!

If you would like to get an advanced copy before it goes live, go to oceanbreezea dventures.net

See you there!

Chapter Thirteen

Appendix I:

Contact Information Car Rental Companies

When it comes to exploring the picturesque landscapes of Hawaii, having a reliable rental car is key to unlocking the full potential of your adventure. Here are some trusted options for car rental in Hawaii:

- HawaiiCar Rental

- **Little Hawaii Rent A Car**

  - Phone: (808) 374-2137

- AirportOn Airport Companies at Honolulu International

  - Budget: 808-836-1700

  - Dollar: 866-434-2226

  - Enterprise: 844-913-0737

  - Hertz: 808-837-7100

  - National: 844-913-0738

  - Avis: 808-834-5536

- ◦ Alamo: 844-913-0736

- ◦ Thrifty: 877-283-0898

- ◦ Sixt: 808-650-2007

- AirportOff-Airport Car Rentals at Kahului

  - ◦ Avis: 808-871-7576

  - ◦ Budget: 808-871-8811, ext 242

  - ◦ Dollar: 808-877-2732

  - ◦ Enterprise: 808-871-1511

  - ◦ Hertz: 808-893-5200

  - ◦ National: 808-871-8852

  - ◦ Alamo: 808-872-1470

- AirportOff-Airport Car Rentals at Kahului

  - ◦ Rent-A-Car: 808-872-1470

  - ◦ Avis Rent-A-Car: 808-871-7576

  - ◦ Budget Rent-A-Car: 808-871-8811, ext 242

  - ◦ Dollar Rent-A-Car: 808-877-2732

  - ◦ Enterprise Rent-A-Car: 808-871-1511

  - ◦ Hertz Rent-A-Car: 808-893-5200

  - ◦ National Rent-A-Car: 808-871-8852

Ensure a smooth journey by verifying the contact information directly with the car rental companies, as details may be subject to change. Happy exploring!

Made in the USA
Las Vegas, NV
23 April 2024

89058853R00079